GLUTEN-FREE
COOKING
for Kids

GLUTEN-FREE
COOKING
for Kids

PHIL VICKERY

Photography by Kate Whitaker

METRO BOOKS
New York

Project editor: Jennifer Wheatley
Photographer: Kate Whitaker
Designer: Jacqui Caulton
Food stylist: Annie Rigg
Home economist for recipe development:
Bea Harling
Props stylist: Lisa Harrison
Copy editor: Jane Bamforth
Americanizer: Lee Faber
Production: Gemma John and Nic Jones

Acknowledgments

Well, as usual, where do I start? Kyle, thanks again
for another chance—I appreciate your support over
the years. I'd like to thank the following people: my
agents John Rush and Luigi Bonomi, who make all
this seamless; Jenny, fab job again, and good luck
with the baby; all the production crew, Estella Hung
for her editorial assistance, Jacqui Caulton for her
superb design, Kate Whitaker for the use of her home
and lovely photos, Lisa Harrison for the props—love
them; Jane Bamforth, sorry for all the mistakes and
bad grammar; Annie Rigg, Rachel Wood, and Bea
Harling, the home economists—you are all brilliant—
and all at Coeliac UK for your support and help, but
in particular Jo Archer for checking all the recipes
and content. Also a thanks to Benedicte Ennis for her
invaluable help in testing the recipes, and for the loan
of her beautiful children as models; and Mairead at
Lavida foods for all the gluten-free pasta. Finally, I
dedicate this book to all celiacs. My heart goes out to
you and I hope this helps in some small way.

CONTENTS

FOREWORD

The diagnosis of celiac disease can seem daunting, especially for a child, but there is no reason why children can't go on to lead full and happy gluten-free lives.

Studies show that if a family member is diagnosed with celiac disease, there is a one in ten chance of a close relative developing or having the disease, so it is important to highlight celiac disease in your family with your family doctor and make sure everyone is tested for the condition, particularly if your child is having symptoms.

Those children who are diagnosed may have been unwell for some time, and made a mental connection between feeling unwell and food. It is important to get them interested in food again, and help them understand that this new, gluten-free food will help them get better.

Once a child is on the gluten-free diet, there are a lot of firsts and hurdles to get through. The learning curve will steepen for you both as your child goes to school, eats at children's parties, has a meal at a friend's house, and so on.

All of these hurdles can be overcome with communication and educating those who are going to cook for your child. Working with people to explain ingredients and how to use them in a safe environment will help you feel more comfortable, and keep your child healthy.

It may be difficult for your child to understand, at first, why they can't eat what their friends are eating. This can have an impact socially, and it is important to make sure they understand the reasons behind it, so that they take responsibility for their own diet.

Having a child with celiac disease can often seem as though it is harder for the parent, as there are so many situations when it feels like you aren't in control. Talking to your child and helping them understand their condition and their diet is essential. By opening up communication about this, you, as their parent, will begin to feel more comfortable that your child is living gluten-free, even when they're not with you.

Equipping them to continue their life gluten-free when away from home and eating out is the next hurdle, and simple steps can make sure that your child is aware of cross-contamination and which ingredients to use.

Above all, gluten-free food can be tasty and fun, and getting your child interested in eating it and cooking it will be a rewarding experience.

Coeliac UK

INTRODUCTION

What is celiac disease?

Celiac disease (pronounced seeliac) is often misunderstood. It is frequently regarded as an allergy or simple food intolerance, but it is actually a lifelong, autoimmune disease affecting the gut and other parts of the body. The body's immune system reacts to the gluten in food, so it attacks itself when gluten is eaten. Gluten is a protein found in wheat, barley, and rye, and some people are also affected by oats. Gluten gives bread its elasticity, and cakes their "spring."

People with celiac disease are sensitive to gluten when it is eaten. The small intestine is lined with tiny finger-like projections called villi. These play a crucial role in digestion as they increase the surface area of the small intestine, and allow essential nutrients to be absorbed from food into the blood stream. However, for people with celiac disease, when gluten comes into contact with the villi, it triggers a response by the immune system which attacks the villi as if they were a "foreign" substance. The villi very quickly become damaged and inflamed, and cannot extract key nutrients from the food we eat. This results in a range of different problems with varying severity.

What are the symptoms?

There is a variety of gastrointestinal symptoms such as cramps, bloating, flatulence, and diarrhea. It is quite common for these to be confused with the symptoms of irritable bowel syndrome (IBS), and only later to be identified as resulting from celiac disease.

In children, common symptoms include muscle wasting in the arms and legs, bloated tummy, irritability, and failure to gain weight or loss of weight after previously growing well. Symptoms in older children vary as they do in adults.

The risk of developing long-term problems like osteoporosis (porous/weakened bones) is reduced if you are diagnosed as a child, as the gluten-free diet allows the gut to heal, and absorption of calcium, essential for strong bones, returns to normal.

Typical symptoms

Symptoms of celiac disease vary in severity. Most symptoms stem from the malabsorption of nutrients, and include diarrhea, fatigue, and iron deficiency, but there is a range of other symptoms, such as:

- Bloating
- Abdominal pains
- Nausea
- Diarrhea
- Tiredness
- Headaches
- Weight loss (but not in all cases)

- Mouth ulcers
- Hair loss
- Skin rash
- Defective tooth enamel
- Problems with fertility
- Recurrent miscarriages

Symptoms of celiac disease in infants include:

- Diarrhea
- Stools often yellow and foul-smelling
- Lower-than-expected weight gain
- General unhappiness
- Muscle wastage
- Abdominal swelling
- Poor appetite

How do I get my child diagnosed?

First, if you suspect your child may have celiac disease, don't panic! Just remember, it is entirely manageable with a controlled diet.

There is a clear procedure for diagnosing celiac disease. The first thing to do is talk through your child's symptoms with your family doctor as they can perform a simple blood test. This test looks for antibodies which are produced in response to eating gluten. **It is important to make sure your child is following a normal diet leading up to the test, as they need to have the antibodies in their blood for the test to work, and these will only be there if they have been eating gluten.** It is quite common for people to go undiagnosed if they have followed a gluten-free diet for a number of days or weeks before having the test, as the immune system will be producing fewer antibodies. This will give a false negative result to the test. To get an accurate test result, it is important to consume food that contains gluten, daily, for a minimum of six weeks before blood is being taken for the test.

If the test is positive, it is recommended that people then have an intestinal biopsy which examines the appearance of the villi in the small intestine under a microscope to check for damage. This will confirm the diagnosis, which your child needs before starting on a lifelong gluten-free diet. Again, the biopsy of the small intestine must be done while they're following a gluten-based diet, and will usually be performed under a general anaesthetic or sedation. If your child is already following a gluten-free diet when they have their biopsy, it might show a completely normal intestinal lining or they may have an inconclusive result.

What is the treatment?

Celiac disease is treated with a gluten-free diet, and means that wheat, barley, rye, and derived ingredients must all be avoided. The most obvious sources of gluten in the diet are pastas, cereals, breads, flours, pizza bases, pastry, cakes, crackers, and cookies. Oats can sometimes be contaminated with other grains, and although most people with celiac disease are able to tolerate uncontaminated oats without a problem, others may be sensitive, and should avoid them. Uncontaminated oats are available, but should be tried under the supervision of your child's healthcare team.

Following a strict gluten-free diet allows the intestines to heal, and alleviates symptoms in most cases. Being diagnosed early in life can also eliminate the increased risk of osteoporosis and intestinal cancer that accompanies long-term celiac disease.

You will need to be careful that your child is following their gluten-free diet, and that they understand what might happen if they don't. Be sure you make the nursery or school aware of their diet, so that you can avoid your child swapping food or eating things they shouldn't.

It is important to explain to children what celiac disease is, what gluten does to their bodies, and what foods they should avoid, and answer any questions they might have about their condition.

Coeliac UK, the British national charity for people with celiac disease, provides information for children including a special booklet, "Me and My Tummy," designed for children up to seven years. It explains celiac disease and how it affects the body in easy-to-understand words and using bright and colorful pictures. The booklet can also be used as an educational tool in schools and nurseries. The US charity Celiac Disease Foundation (www.celiac.org) also has a variety of helpful booklets.

It is also important to explain celiac disease to the whole family, including siblings, so they understand why their brother or sister needs to eat different foods.

What can my child eat?

There is plenty of food that is naturally gluten-free, and can be included in a gluten-free diet. In particular, carbohydrate-rich foods such as potatoes, rice, and corn do not contain gluten. All fresh meat, poultry, and fish, all fresh fruit and vegetables, fresh herbs, individual spices, dried legumes, rice noodles, plain nuts, eggs, dairy products, sugar, honey, oils and vinegars, vanilla extract, and fresh and dried yeast are suitable. In fact, the gluten-free diet has the potential to be one of the healthiest diets around because of the increased emphasis placed upon eating fresh, natural, and unprocessed food. If undiagnosed celiac disease has resulted in the poor absorption of vitamins and minerals, a gluten-free diet should soon restore this to healthy levels, and lead to a feeling of health and well-being.

More and more manufacturers are producing gluten-free substitute foods, such as gluten-free bread, crackers, and pasta, some of which are just as good as their gluten-containing equivalents. The Celiac Sprue Association (CSA) publishes a gluten-free book, called *The Celiac's Best Friend.* You may need to experiment to find products that your child is happy to eat. Some manufacturers are happy to send out free samples for you to try if you ask them.

Food labels

Look at the food label and read the ingredient list to see if the product contains gluten. However, be careful as food labeling with allergy advice is a recommendation in the US, but not compulsory and whereas manufacturers have to declare if a product contains wheat, it might also contain barley, rye, or oats. Therefore use food labels as a guideline but, if you are in any doubt, avoid products you are unsure about.

Foods that are naturally gluten-free:

- All fresh meat and fish
- All fresh fruit and vegetables
- Fresh herbs and individual spices
- Corn and cornmeal (polenta)
- Dried legumes (peas, lentils and beans)
- Rice and wild rice
- Rice bran
- Rice noodles
- Plain nuts and seeds
- Eggs
- Dairy products (milk, cream, plain yogurt, cheese)
- Soybeans and plain tofu
- Sugar
- Honey
- Corn syrup
- Maple syrup
- Molasses
- Jams and marmalade
- Pure oils and fats
- Vinegars (except malt vinegar)
- Tomato paste
- Vanilla extract
- Fresh and dried yeast

Foods and drinks that often contain gluten which you need to check:

- Baking powder
- Communion wafers
- Corn tortillas—these may also include gluten-containing flour
- Frozen French fries—these may be coated with gluten-containing flour
- Bouillon cubes/powder
- Vegetable soup—this may contain pearl barley
- Seasoning mixes
- Mustard products
- Packaged suet – this may have flour in it to stop it sticking together
- Commercial salad dressings and sauces
- Soy sauce (there are gluten-free brands available)
- Dry-roasted nuts
- Pretzels
- Bombay mix
- Food that has been deep-fried with other gluten-containing food, e.g., battered fish and chips
- Flavored potato chips
- Some sparkling drinks (alcoholic or non-alcoholic) may contain barley flour to give a cloudy appearance
- Coffee from vending machines
- Malted-milk drinks
- Barley water or flavored barley water

Gluten-free alternatives

In general, it is a good idea to be wary of cereals if you are cooking for a gluten-free diet, yet there are a number of naturally gluten-free varieties that are worth knowing about. These give a similar result to cooking with regular flour and cereals, and allow you to try recipes that are otherwise out of bounds. As with all other foods, it is best to approach with a degree of caution. Alternative, gluten-free grains include:

- Arrowroot
- Buckwheat flour
- Potato flour
- Carob powder
- Chestnut flour
- Cornstarch
- Chickpea flour (Gram flour)
- Cornmeal (Polenta)
- Flaxseed

- Lotus-root powder
- Potato flour
- Quinoa flour
- Rice flour
- Sago
- Sorghum flour
- Soy flour
- Tapioca flour (Cassava flour)
- Teff flour

Other useful ingredients

Xanthan gum is produced by fermentation and is a natural type of starch. It improves the texture and shelf life of baked products. When added to gluten-free flour mixes (see page 19), it replaces the gluten "stretch factor." It works like gluten by binding ingredients during the baking process to give a conventional texture. It can be bought at health food shops, and comes in a powder form that dissolves easily in water. Xanthan gum should be combined with your gluten-free flour mix before adding any liquid.

What about contamination?

Unfortunately, even the tiniest amount of gluten can cause problems for people with celiac disease. Dry, gluten-containing ingredients like flour and bread crumbs are high-risk ingredients for contamination when you are producing gluten-free meals. It is a good idea to keep gluten-free foods separate in the kitchen to make sure you avoid contamination with gluten from other foods. Steps to avoid contamination include:

- cleaning surfaces immediately before their use

- using clean oil for frying potatoes and gluten-free foods—do NOT reuse oil that has been used for cooking breaded or battered products

- keeping all pans, utensils, and colanders separate during food preparation and cooking
- using a clean broiler, separate toaster, or toaster bags to make gluten-free toast
- making sure that butter, spreads, jams, pickles, chutneys, and sauces are not contaminated with bread crumbs
- using squeeze bottles to help avoid contamination through the dipping of spoons or knives.

Food safety and hygiene is important especially when you are cooking for babies and young children. For more information on food safety and hygiene, visit the websites: http://www.foodsafety.gov and http://www.nhs.uk/LiveWell/Homehygiene/Pages/Homehygienehub.aspx.

Cooking for your child

Children on a gluten-free diet can still enjoy really delicious, flavorful food. In fact, a gluten-free diet not only offers the chance to improve the quality of the food you eat by cooking with fresh, unprocessed ingredients, but also helps to introduce your taste buds to new flavor combinations. The recipes in this book are all about opening out the gluten-free diet—giving your child food to enjoy, food that is nutritious, and food that will make them feel seriously good!

Babies and toddlers

You will not know your child has celiac disease until they start eating gluten. Weaning onto solid foods usually happens between four and seven months of age and it is recommended that you introduce gluten into the diet from six months onwards. If your baby is diagnosed at this early age, suitable first foods include puréed fruit and vegetables, and gluten-free cereals such as baby rice. Ready-prepared baby foods are made to strict guidelines to cater for all the nutritional requirements of babies' first solid foods. From about eight or nine months of age, babies can start eating normal foods such as small gluten-free sandwiches, pasta, breakfast cereals, desserts, and cooked vegetables.

School-age kids

As your child starts or changes school, you should arrange a meeting with the appropriate members of staff to tell them about your child's needs. Catering for a child with celiac disease doesn't necessarily mean preparing specific gluten-free food. Even small changes in practice can ensure the food cooked is safe—for example, frying potatoes in separate oil.

Schools are required to provide gluten-free meals if celiac diagnosis has been made by a doctor, although some schools may require more information than others. If your child needs a packed lunch for school, there are plenty of gluten-free options in this book to try to make with your child, or check the Celiac Societies websites (see Directory, page 156) for ideas.

Teenagers

As your child gets older, they will be more likely to eat and cook with friends, and eat outside the home. Teaching your children some basic cooking skills, and trying out a few recipes in this book with them will give them the confidence to cook for themselves when they do leave home. If they are worried about eating out, cooking a gluten-free meal for a group of friends using some of these recipes can be a great way to explain to friends about the gluten-free diet. (See Cooking on Their Own, pages 86–109).

Eating out

Maintaining a gluten-free diet while out and about can often feel like a real challenge. Some restaurants will advertise that they cater for people with celiac disease, so it is worth checking their website before you go. Calling ahead can also help as places will often be happy to make adjustments to meals if they are given notice. You should always check at a restaurant or eatery if their usual menu items can be adjusted to make them right for a gluten-free diet as this can often mean there is more that is safe to eat than you think. Ask the waiting staff to check with the chef, and if you're not sure, you could ask to speak to the chef yourself. Most places will be happy to accommodate you, and therefore eating out on a gluten-free diet shouldn't be a barrier to managing your child's gluten-free lifestyle.

Children's birthday parties

If your child is going to someone else's party, it's worth bearing in mind that the party organizer will probably be very busy, so don't automatically expect them to cater for your child. Ask what types of party food are being prepared and consider substituting similar gluten-free versions. Perhaps you could bring along gluten-free alternatives for everyone to try so that your child feels included. If the party is taking place at an activity center, it's worth calling the center beforehand to check what food is provided as part of the party package, as it isn't normally gluten-free.

NOTES ON THE RECIPES

- No salt is added to recipes for babies. For all recipes, salt is an optional seasoning.

- Generally aim to give younger children the same food as all in the family are eating; and vary the texture to suit your child e.g., soft, puréed, thicker-textured or finger food pieces. Slow cookers are very useful here to provide soft-textured meats, and for adapting family meals. For babies and toddlers, introduce individual vegetable or fruit purées to start with, sieved and super smooth. Then try combinations in recipes. There's no barrier to flavors; just note your health professional's advice about salt, common allergens, and ingredients.

- Add liquid to fruit and vegetables to make a softer mash or purée. This can be water, or milk and water. Homemade (no added salt) stocks are useful to make a thinner texture (see page 18).

Oven temperatures and cooking times

The oven should be preheated. All appliances vary in performance, especially convection ovens and microwaves. Adjust the temperature and the cooking time according to the type of oven you own.

Portion sizes

Babies, toddlers, and children all vary in the amount they eat. Rather than give a precise portion size for each recipe, I have opted for a family approach: serving sizes are given as four adult portions. To be practical, you can adapt the amounts to suit the needs of your family. For example, a serving size of four can be divided into two adult portions, two smaller children's portions (making up one adult portion), and a remaining adult portion to be frozen and saved for another meal. I've aimed to minimize separating children's food from family food. The baby vegetable purées (pages 22–26), for instance, can also be served as side dishes for adults.

Successful gluten-free baking

- Measure ingredients accurately and use the correct pan size.

- Have ingredients at room temperature when you start.

- The amount of liquid needed may differ depending on the brand or type of flours you use. Generally you tend to need a wetter-than-normal mixture before baking and may have to adjust the quantity of liquid given in the recipe—go by the description of the texture (for example, soft and dropping, wet, or for pouring into the pan).

- If not enough liquid is added, the finished result can be disappointing and heavy in texture. Mixtures tend to stiffen on standing and soak up the moisture further, so be sure to mix and bake immediately, especially when you are using baking powder.

BASIC RECIPES

Chicken stock

MAKES: ABOUT 1 QUART
PREPARATION: 10 MINUTES
COOKING: ABOUT 2 HOURS

2 medium onions

1 leek

2 medium carrots

2 celery stalks

1 cooked or raw chicken carcass

small bunch of fresh herbs
(such as bay, thyme, parsley)

freshly ground black pepper

Roughly chop the onions, leek, carrots, and celery stalks.

Put all the ingredients into a large pan with 2 quarts water. Bring to a boil, skim the surface, and then partially cover and simmer gently for about 2 hours.

Strain the stock through a sieve and cool quickly.

HINTS

- Check the flavor and adjust the amount of liquid if necessary at the end of cooking.
- The stock has no salt added, so is suitable to use in baby food.

To store: Keep in the fridge for up to 3 days.
To freeze: Once the stock has cooled, freeze in airtight containers in small portions. Defrost completely before reheating thoroughly.

Vegetable stock

MAKES: ABOUT 1 QUART
PREPARATION: 10 MINUTES
COOKING: ABOUT 1 HOUR

2 medium onions

1 garlic clove

2 mushrooms or a few pieces of
dried mushroom, optional

1 leek

2 medium carrots

2 celery stalks

small bunch of fresh herbs (such as
bay, thyme, parsley)

freshly ground black pepper

Roughly chop the onions, garlic, mushrooms, leek, carrots, and celery. Put all the ingredients into a large pan with 1½ quarts water. Bring to a boil, and then partially cover and simmer gently for about 1 hour.

Strain the stock through a sieve and cool quickly.

HINT

- The stock has no salt added, so is suitable to use in baby food—it is very useful for thinning purées.

To store: Keep in the fridge for up to 3 days.
To freeze: Once the stock has cooled, freeze in airtight containers, in small portions. Defrost completely before reheating thoroughly.

Gluten-free flour mix A

MAKES: 7¼ CUPS (2¼ LB)
PREPARATION: 5 MINUTES

5¼ cups (25 oz) fine white rice flour

1 cup (7 oz) potato flour

1 cup (3½ oz) tapioca flour

Mix all the flours together very thoroughly, or put into a food processor and pulse until mixed. Store in an airtight container and use by the soonest "best before" date on your packaged flour.

Gluten-free flour mix B

MAKES: 8¼ CUPS (2¼ LB)
PREPARATION: 5 MINUTES

2½ cups (10½ oz) fine cornmeal
　(polenta) or chestnut flour

4¼ cups (18 oz) brown rice flour

1½ cups (7 oz) cornstarch

Mix all the flours together very thoroughly, or put into a food processor and pulse until mixed. Store in an airtight container and use by the soonest "best before" date on your packaged flour.

Short pastry

MAKES: 1 X 1½-INCH DEEP, 9½-INCH
ROUND TART CRUST
PREPARATION: 10 MINUTES
BAKING: 15–20 MINUTES

2¼ cups (8 oz) Gluten-free Flour Mix
　A (see above)

1 teaspoon xanthan gum

2 pinches of salt

½ cup (4 oz) margarine

1 large egg, beaten, at room
　temperature

Place the flour, xanthan gum, and salt in a mixing bowl, and combine really well. Rub in the margarine until you have achieved the consistency of fine bread crumbs. Add the egg and a little water, and mix well. Keep an eye on the texture—you may need to add a little more water so it is nice and soft; bear in mind the xanthan gum will tighten up the mixture considerably. Roll out and use as required.

To make a tart crust: Roll out the pastry to a circle, approximately 12 inches in diameter, on a cornstarch-dusted work surface. Transfer the pastry to a 1½-inch deep, 9½-inch round pan and line with baking parchment and dried beans. Bake for 10 minutes at 350°F, then reduce the temperature to 325°F for 10–15 minutes.

Carefully lift out the baking parchment and beans, brush thickly with beaten egg, covering any cracks, and return to the oven for 5–6 minutes to just set the egg. Brush with egg again, and bake for another 5 minutes. To store, wrap the dough in plastic wrap and refrigerate for up to 2 days. Do not freeze.

Baby Food

I have had many letters and emails over the past few years from moms and dads who have found out that their children have celiac disease. Whether they had never really cooked before, or were experienced home cooks, all of them asked about gluten-free baby food. So, with this in mind, I decided to develop recipes to help. What I offer here may look very simple, but I have tried to incorporate texture and color into all the recipes to make them appealing, and give your child the best possible start in life.

Roasted pepper and squash purée

Love the color and flavor profile here. The roasting process really concentrates the flavors of this.

SERVES: 4
PREPARATION: 10 MINUTES
COOKING: 30–40 MINUTES

2 yellow or orange peppers, seeded and cut into 1–1¼-inch chunks

2 red peppers, seeded and cut into 1–1¼-inch chunks

2 cups (9 oz) squash flesh, e.g., butternut, cut into 1–1¼-inch chunks

2 tablespoons olive oil

Preheat the oven to 375°F.

Spread the vegetables out onto a large baking pan, drizzle with the olive oil and turn the vegetables to coat them. Roast for about 30–40 minutes, until soft. Turn the vegetables over halfway through.

Purée the vegetables in a blender with a little water if necessary.

HINTS

- You can use sweet potato or yam, instead of the squash.
- The purée can be made chunkier for toddlers.

To store: Keep in the fridge for up to 3 days and reheat thoroughly before serving.

To freeze: Cool and transfer to ice cube trays to freeze in convenient portions. Defrost completely before reheating thoroughly.

Corn, potato and apple broth

A nice easy broth with a bit of body, and with a slightly sweet apple edge.

SERVES: 4
PREPARATION: 20 MINUTES
COOKING: 25–35 MINUTES

4 tablespoons extra-virgin olive oil

1 medium onion, finely chopped

1 garlic clove, chopped

2 small sweet potatoes or yams, chopped into small chunks

2 small potatoes, chopped into small chunks

1 small apple, pared, cored, and roughly chopped

1 cup canned corn kernels, drained

generous 2 cups (17 fl oz) vegetable stock (use a gluten-free, reduced-salt vegetable bouillon cube or homemade stock, page 18)

freshly ground black pepper

Heat the oil in a large pan, then add the onion and garlic. Cook for 5 minutes to soften and take on a little color.

Next add the potato chunks, apple, corn kernels and stock, and bring to a boil. Season with pepper, then turn down the heat, partially cover, and gently simmer for 20–30 minutes or until all the ingredients are soft.

Once the vegetables are cooked and very soft, mash them roughly with a potato masher, until you have a thickish, chunky purée.

HINTS

- You can serve this on its own, or with cooked meat: pork goes very well with the apple flavor.
- Alternatively, add some finely chopped, freshly cooked chicken.

To store: Keep in the fridge for up to 2 days and reheat thoroughly before serving.

To freeze: Cool and freeze in an airtight container. Defrost completely before reheating thoroughly.

Spinach, zucchini, and pea purée

I think it's essential that you introduce color and texture early to children. So here is a vibrant green vegetable purée.

SERVES: 4
PREPARATION: 10 MINUTES
COOKING: 10 MINUTES

1¼ cups (10 fl oz) vegetable stock (use a gluten-free, reduced-salt vegetable bouillon cube or homemade stock, page 18)
²/₃ cup peas, fresh or frozen
1¼ cups zucchini, finely sliced
6 large handfuls (10½ oz) baby leaf spinach

Heat the stock in a pan and cook the peas and zucchini for 5–10 minutes, or until tender. Add the spinach leaves for the last 5 minutes. Drain and reserve the stock.

Blend the vegetables with enough reserved stock to make a smooth purée, using a hand-held blender or food processor.

HINTS

- Any combination of green vegetables works well.
- For baby's first food, push a portion of the purée through a sieve.
- For adults, add a little seasoning and serve as a side dish.

To store: Keep in the fridge for up to 3 days and reheat thoroughly before serving.

To freeze: Cool and transfer to ice cube trays to freeze in convenient portions. Defrost completely before reheating thoroughly.

Root vegetable purée

Root vegetables are an excellent way of adding texture to your child's diet. They can also be a good substitute for potatoes or rice.

SERVES: 4
PREPARATION: 10 MINUTES
COOKING: 20-25 MINUTES

1 tablespoon vegetable oil
1 small onion, finely chopped
1 medium sweet potato or yam, sliced
2 parsnips, sliced and woody core removed
1 carrot, sliced
generous 2 cups (17 fl oz) vegetable stock (use a gluten-free, reduced-salt vegetable bouillon cube or homemade stock, page 18) or water
roasted beet fingers, to serve

Heat the oil in a pan and cook the onion until soft. Add the root vegetables, pour in the stock and cook for about 15–20 minutes or until the vegetables are soft. Drain and reserve the stock. Blend all the vegetables with enough reserved stock to make a purée, using a hand-held blender or food processor. Serve with roasted beet fingers. To make these, slice whole beets into fingers, drizzle with a little oil and roast in the oven at 400°F for about 20 minutes.

HINTS

- Try introducing different tastes by adding rutabaga or celeriac.
- For older children, lightly mash the vegetables instead of puréeing.
- For adults, add a little seasoning or Moroccan spices (such as ground cumin, ground coriander, ginger, or turmeric) and serve as a side dish.

To store: Keep in the fridge for up to 3 days and reheat thoroughly before serving.

To freeze: Cool and transfer to ice cube trays to freeze in convenient portions. Defrost completely before reheating thoroughly.

Creamy carrot and lentil dhal

This is mildly spiced for babies. Tinker with the spices if you want a more adult accompaniment: I would add crushed garlic and equal pinches of fennel, mustard and fenugreek seeds in with the onions, and then finish with a squeeze of lime, and some fresh coriander.

1 tablespoon canola or olive oil

2 medium carrots, diced

1 small onion, finely diced

pinch of ground cumin

pinch of ground turmeric

6 tablespoons red lentils

1¼ cups (10 fl oz) vegetable stock (use a gluten-free, reduced-salt vegetable bouillon cube or homemade stock, page 18)

1 tablespoon plain yogurt, optional

Heat the oil in a medium pan and sauté the carrots and onion with the spices for a few minutes. Stir in the lentils and stock, then simmer for approximately 20 minutes or until the lentils and vegetables are soft. Add more water if necessary, but leave it quite thick.

Blend the mixture using a hand-held blender or food processor. Stir the yogurt in at the end, if using.

HINT
- The yogurt is optional, in case of sensitivity to dairy foods.

To store: Keep in the fridge for up to 3 days and reheat thoroughly before serving.

To freeze: Cool and transfer to ice cube trays to freeze in convenient portions. Defrost completely before reheating thoroughly.

Roast chicken Sunday lunch broth

Another nice, simple recipe. All the quantities are approximate (as most of them are leftovers), so it's really an "anything goes" meal.

1¼ cups onions, diced or sliced

Heaping cup roast potatoes, diced or sliced

1 heaping cup cooked carrots, diced or sliced

2 cups cooked green cabbage, diced or sliced

2 cups cooked broccoli, diced or sliced

1 gluten-free, reduced-salt chicken bouillon cube

2 tablespoons rice or any gluten-free pasta

2 cups roast chicken, sliced

1 tablespoon red currant jelly, optional

Place the diced or sliced vegetables in a large pan with 1 quart water, the crumbled bouillon cube, and the rice or pasta. Bring to a boil. Turn down the heat, partially cover, and simmer for about 30 minutes.

Once cooked, add the chicken, and heat through for 5 minutes.

For babies, blend to make a purée, using a hand-held blender or food processor. For adults, leave chunky, if you like.

To serve, spoon into a deep bowl. Add a little red currant jelly, if using, and swirl through.

HINT

- This is good for babies, children, and adults alike; the only difference being the consistency of the purée.

To store: Keep in the fridge for up to 3 days and reheat thoroughly before serving.

To freeze: Cool and transfer to ice-cube trays to freeze in convenient portions. Defrost completely before reheating thoroughly.

Basic vegetable broth

Here's a good basic broth or soup—just add more or less water; it's up to you. I like it quite thick, so just cover the vegetables with water. You can also add a little gluten-free pasta at the same time as the vegetables.

1 onion, roughly chopped

1½ cups zucchini, roughly chopped

1 leek, roughly chopped

2 medium carrots, roughly chopped

¾ cup frozen peas

3 cups cauliflower, cut into small florets

1¼ cups broccoli, cut into small florets

1 gluten-free, reduced-salt vegetable bouillon cube

2 tablespoons olive oil

freshly ground black pepper

Place all the vegetables into a large pan. Just cover with cold water and add the crumbled bouillon cube.

Bring to a boil, turn down the heat, and simmer for about 30 minutes (do not overcook).

When the vegetables are soft, add the olive oil and plenty of pepper. Blitz in a food processor or with a hand-held blender.

HINTS

- A tablespoon of quinoa added into the pan with the vegetables gives this vegetarian dish some protein.
- Alternatively, poach some chopped chicken or turkey breast in with the basic broth, to vary.

To store: Keep in the fridge for up to 3 days and reheat thoroughly before serving.

To freeze: Cool and transfer to ice-cube trays to freeze in convenient portions. Defrost completely before reheating thoroughly.

Autumn vegetable stew with white beans and chard

Packed full of flavor, this is a great soupy broth for babies or toddlers, and adults will enjoy it too.

1 quart vegetable stock (use a gluten-free, reduced-salt vegetable bouillon cube or homemade stock, page 18)

¼ cup quinoa, soaked overnight in cold water and drained

1 large onion, chopped

2 small carrots, chopped

1 leek, finely sliced

15-oz can cannellini beans, drained

2-4 garlic cloves, crushed

4 large handfuls (7 oz) Swiss chard or spinach, finely chopped

3¼ cups green cabbage, finely sliced

2 tablespoons olive oil

2 tablespoons chopped fresh mint

Place the bouillon, quinoa, onion, carrots, leek, beans, and garlic into a pan. Partially cover and simmer gently for about 20 minutes until the quinoa is cooked. Stir occasionally; you may need to top up with boiling water.

Once soft, add the chard and cabbage and simmer for another 10–15 minutes. When the stew has reduced and is nicely thickened, add the oil and mint.

Transfer to a food processor and blitz to the required texture.

HINTS

- Poach some chopped chicken or turkey breast in with the basic broth, to vary.

To store: Keep in the fridge for up to 3 days and reheat thoroughly before serving.

To freeze: Cool and transfer to ice cube trays to freeze in convenient portions. Defrost completely before reheating thoroughly.

Three fruit purées

These purées can be eaten fresh or you could freeze them in ice pop molds or ice cube trays and serve as little ice pops or frozen desserts (see page 52).

Berry purée

SERVES: 4
PREPARATION: 5 MINUTES

2 cups mixed berries, such as strawberries, raspberries, and blackberries

Purée the fruit in a blender and then sieve to remove the seeds.

HINT

• Use any combination of fresh and frozen berries.

To store: Keep in the fridge for up to 2 days.

To freeze: Transfer to ice pop molds or ice cube trays to freeze in convenient portions.

Mango and pineapple purée

SERVES: 4
PREPARATION: 5 MINUTES

1 small fresh mango, cut into chunks
2 cups fresh pineapple chunks

Purée the fruit in a blender.

HINT

• The pineapple retains some texture and may not be completely smooth after blending, so this purée is best for older babies.

To store: Keep in the fridge for up to 2 days.

To freeze: Transfer to ice pop molds or ice cube trays to freeze in convenient portions.

Pear and apple purée

SERVES: 4
PREPARATION: 5 MINUTES
COOKING: 10–15 MINUTES

4 pears, pared, cored and chopped
2 medium dessert apples, pared, cored, and sliced
squeeze of lemon juice

Put all the ingredients into a small pan, add 2 tablespoons water, and bring to a simmer. Cover and cook gently for 10–15 minutes until soft. Purée the fruit in a blender, or mash with a fork.

To store: Keep in the fridge for up to 2 days.

To freeze: Transfer to ice pop molds or ice cube trays to freeze in convenient portions.

Toddler Food

Many worried parents have contacted me for advice on feeding their kids. The recipes in this section are simple to cook, and their ingredients easy to shop for. I have tried to incorporate lots of color, and most importantly, taste. As in all the recipes, I have cut down on salt and sugar, and replaced these with vinegars, citrus flavors such as lemon or lime, herbs, and subtle spices. There are a lot of braises and bakes and they all freeze well, making your job easy.

SERVES: 6–8
PREPARATION: 15 MINUTES
COOKING: 25–30 MINUTES

Easy mixed vegetable hash with tangy salad

A tasty way of getting plenty of vegetables into a meal, plus a crunchy salad on the side. Instead of cooking the vegetables from scratch, you can also make this with any leftovers—just use whatever you have.

FOR THE HASH

2 medium potatoes, chopped into 1-inch cubes

3 small carrots, chopped into 1-inch cubes

½ medium cauliflower, broken into bite-sized florets

4 tablespoons olive oil

1 medium onion, chopped into 1-inch chunks

1 gluten-free, reduced-salt chicken bouillon cube

freshly ground black pepper

FOR THE SALAD

4 cups mixed lettuce leaves

2 small McIntosh apples, unpared

2 tablespoons olive oil

Cook the potatoes and carrots in a pan of boiling water for 5 minutes. Add the cauliflower florets, and cook until all the vegetables are tender. Drain and set aside.

Heat the olive oil in a large nonstick frying pan. Add the onion, and cook for a few minutes to brown slightly.

Next add the cooked potatoes, carrots, and cauliflower, and continue to cook until they all take on a little color. Add the crumbled bouillon cube, ⅔ cup water and a generous grinding of pepper.

Stir well, and cook over high heat, so the bouillon cube dissolves, and the liquid reduces slightly: this will make the dish nice and moist, but not wet. Check the seasoning, and adjust if needed.

To make the salad, place the lettuce into a large bowl. Coarsely grate the apples and mix into the lettuce. Add the olive oil, and mix well again, but do not crush the lettuce. Serve the hash with the salad.

HINT

- If your child does not like the texture of the hash, the mix can be whizzed to make it less chunky, or puréed completely in a food processor.

To store: Keep the hash in the fridge for up to 2 days and reheat thoroughly before serving.

To freeze: Cool the hash, and freeze in an airtight container. Defrost completely before reheating thoroughly.

SERVES: 6–8
PREPARATION: 10 MINUTES
COOKING: 20 MINUTES

Braised eggplant and pumpkin with lime, tomatoes, and mint

There's a nice combination of vegetables here. As long as they are really well-cooked and soft, your toddler should enjoy them!

6 tablespoons olive oil

3 medium onions, very finely chopped

1 garlic clove, finely chopped

2 large eggplants, cut into 1-inch chunks

14 oz peeled pumpkin flesh, cut into 2-inch chunks

freshly ground black pepper

1⅓ cups fresh or frozen peas

3 tomatoes, roughly chopped

2 tablespoons chopped fresh mint

juice of 1 large lime

1 tablespoon clear honey

Heat 4 tablespoons of the olive oil in a large frying pan. Add the onions, garlic, eggplant, and pumpkin, mix well, and season with pepper. When the vegetables are sizzling, turn down the heat, cover, and cook for 20 minutes, stirring occasionally, or until they are soft and slightly colored.

Meanwhile, cook the peas in a pan of boiling water. Drain and set aside.

Once the eggplant mixture is cooked, add the cooked peas, the tomatoes, mint, lime juice, and honey and mix well.

Leave to cool, then season with more pepper and the remaining olive oil.

You should end up with a thick stew.

HINTS
- This can be blended with a hand-held blender, or a food processor to make more of a purée.
- This recipe is not recommended for younger babies, because it contains honey, which can cause a rare form of food poisoning in babies under 1 year.

To store: Keep in the fridge for up to 2 days, and reheat thoroughly before serving.

To freeze: Cool and freeze in an airtight container. Defrost completely before reheating thoroughly.

Salmon, tomato, and white fish pie

This version of a favorite classic is adapted for healthier eating with omega-3-rich salmon, plus lower salt and fat.

FOR THE TOMATO SAUCE

1 tablespoon vegetable oil

1 large onion, chopped

2 garlic cloves, chopped

⅓ cup salt-free sun-dried tomatoes, soaked in warm water

14-oz can chopped tomatoes

1 teaspoon red wine vinegar

generous pinch of dark brown sugar

FOR THE FISH

11 oz skinless, boneless white fish, such as coley or pollock

10 oz skinless, boneless salmon

small handful of fresh basil leaves, torn

a few fresh tarragon leaves or chopped dill fronds, optional

FOR THE TOPPING

1 scant cup half-fat crème fraîche

1 tablespoon grated Parmesan cheese

2 cups (about 1 lb) mashed potatoes

1 tablespoon or 1 spray of olive oil

Preheat the oven to 375°F.

First make the tomato sauce. Heat the oil and fry the onion and garlic until golden, about 10 minutes. Stir in the remaining ingredients for the sauce, and cook for another 10–15 minutes to reduce and thicken a little. Spoon the tomato sauce into the base of an ovenproof dish.

Pull any stray bones out of the fish and cut into large chunks. Mix the herbs in with the fish, and arrange it over the tomato sauce.

Dot the fish with spoonfuls of crème fraîche, and sprinkle the Parmesan cheese over. Spoon the mashed potatoes on top, and drizzle or spray the olive oil over the mash. Bake for about 45 minutes, until bubbling, and the fish is cooked through.

HINT

- The tomato sauce can also be served with gluten-free pasta or vegetables.

To store: The pie can be assembled in advance and kept in the fridge for up to 2 days before baking, in which case allow extra time to cook the chilled pie.

To freeze: Chill and freeze the assembled pie before baking. Defrost completely, and bake as above, allowing extra time to cook the chilled pie.

Vegetable curry

I know what you must be thinking: curry and kids? Well, I have found that young children really like the curry profile, provided that it's not too intense. Try adding small amounts of curry spices to begin with, and build them up if your child happily acquires the taste. Serve with gluten-free rice or gluten-free naan if available.

2 tablespoons unsalted butter

1 large onion, thinly sliced

2 garlic cloves, crushed

1 tablespoon mild curry paste or garam masala

1 teaspoon paprika

1 teaspoon ground turmeric

1 teaspoon ground cardamom

pinch of ground cloves, optional

pinch of ground cinnamon

2 medium carrots, cubed

1 medium potato, cubed

2 zucchini, unpared, and chopped into chunks

3½ cups collard greens or spinach, chopped

14-oz can chopped tomatoes

1 scant cup vegetable stock (use a gluten-free, reduced-salt vegetable bouillon cube or homemade stock, page 18)

chopped fresh cilantro leaves, optional

cooked rice or gluten-free naan, to serve

Melt the butter in a large, heavy-based pan and fry the onion, garlic, and curry paste for about 3 minutes. Add the spices and cook, stirring, for 2 minutes more. Add the carrots, potato, zucchini, collard greens or spinach, and cook for 10 minutes, stirring occasionally.

Add the tomatoes and stock, and simmer until the vegetables are soft and reduced a little; about 30 minutes. Add a little water if necessary.

Serve in deep bowls sprinkled with the cilantro.

HINTS

- Add some cubes of paneer (Indian cheese or farmer cheese) to the curry and heat through for 5 minutes at the end.
- This recipe can easily become a chicken curry if pieces of boneless chicken thigh are added to the spices before simmering.
- Vary the vegetables according to what you have available.

To store: Keep in the fridge for up to 3 days and reheat thoroughly before serving.

To freeze: Cool and transfer to an airtight container. Defrost completely before reheating thoroughly.

Pot-roast chicken drumsticks with grapes and crème fraîche

There is something nice about just placing this in front of the kids and letting them help themselves. The spinach can be omitted if you prefer. Any other soft leaf vegetable will also work well, such as collard greens, Napa cabbage or even iceberg or romaine lettuces. Serve with any vegetables that are in season.

3 tablespoons olive oil

8 chicken drumsticks, skin on

1 small onion, chopped

$^2/_3$ cup frozen peas

1 gluten-free, reduced-salt chicken bouillon cube

handful of baby spinach leaves, optional

4–5 tablespoons of half-fat crème fraîche

12–14 seedless green grapes

freshly ground black pepper

Preheat the oven to 375°F.

Heat the oil in a flameproof casserole, add the drumsticks and brown them well on all sides. Season with pepper, and then add the onion and peas.

Stir in $^2/_3$ cup water and the crumbled bouillon cube, and bring to a boil. Cover with a tight-fitting lid, and cook in the oven for 30–45 minutes. To check that the chicken is thoroughly cooked, carefully insert a knife into the thickest part of the meat: if the juices are clear and there is no trace of blood, it is cooked.

Remove from the oven, lift off the lid, and check the seasoning: add the spinach at this point, if using. Stir in the crème fraîche and heat, but do not boil. Finally add the grapes.

To store: This is best eaten immediately.
To freeze: Not suitable.

Sausage, bean, tomato, and potato casserole

A great one-pot meal that's full of the things kids like. This dish is best made the day before, so the flavors develop, then heated through gently in a microwave or low oven.

2 tablespoons vegetable oil

4 gluten-free sausages, halved

1 onion, finely chopped

2 garlic cloves, finely chopped

4 medium potatoes, halved

14-oz can chopped tomatoes

1 tablespoon tomato paste

14-oz can gluten-free baked beans,
   tomato sauce rinsed off

1 gluten-free, reduced-salt beef
   bouillon cube

salt and freshly ground black
   pepper

Preheat the oven to 400°F.

Place a flameproof casserole on the stove and add the vegetable oil, heat, and then add the sausages. Cook until nicely browned on all sides.

Lift out the sausages, and pour off half the fat, then add the onion and stir until nicely browned. This will take about 5 minutes. Add the garlic and stir well.

Add the potatoes, tomatoes, tomato paste, beans, bouillon cube, salt and pepper, and mix well. Finally add a touch of boiling water until you have a nice thick consistency. Bring to a boil, and cover with a tight-fitting lid. Cook in the oven for 35 minutes, or until the potatoes are soft, and starting to fall apart. You may need to re-season at this point.

To store: Keep in the fridge for up to 3 days and reheat thoroughly before serving.

To freeze: Cool and freeze in an airtight container. Defrost completely before reheating thoroughly.

Lamb and quinoa vegetable broth

This is an easy broth to make—the longer it simmers, the better. Instead of quinoa, I sometimes add gluten-free pasta shapes right at the end of the cooking to keep them nice and firm.

1 tablespoon oil

1 lb boneless lamb, cut into small cubes, most fat removed

2 carrots, cut into small cubes

1 leek, sliced

1 onion, chopped

1 small turnip, cut into small pieces

2 celery stalks, sliced

1 quart vegetable stock (use a gluten-free, reduced-salt vegetable bouillon cube or homemade stock, page 18)

⅔ cup quinoa

freshly ground black pepper

chopped fresh parsley, to serve

Heat the oil in a large pan over high heat, and brown the meat all over. Stir in all the vegetables, then the stock and quinoa, and bring to a boil. Turn the heat down, partially cover, and simmer for 1½ hours, or until the lamb is tender. Stir occasionally (remove any scum on the surface) and top up with water if needed.

To serve, add lots of black pepper and sprinkle with the parsley.

HINT

- This cooks really well in a slow cooker. Cook on a low setting and you can leave it bubbling gently for 6–7 hours. Reduce the amount of liquid just to cover the meat and vegetables, as cooking liquid does not evaporate in a slow cooker.

To store: Keep in the fridge for up to 2 days and reheat thoroughly before serving.

To freeze: Cool and freeze in an airtight container. Defrost completely before reheating thoroughly.

Mini apple crumble cheesecakes

A great recipe and really simple to make. My mom often had a large bowl of stewed apples in the fridge and we would always have it with cold custard.

FOR THE APPLE STEW

4 medium Granny Smith apples, pared, cored, and chopped into small pieces

4 tablespoons confectioners' sugar

3 tablespoons apple juice or water

FOR THE CHEESECAKES

⅔ cup gluten-free cream cheese*

⅔ cup Greek yogurt

7-oz can condensed milk

grated zest and juice of 1 lemon

2 gluten-free shortbread cookies*

* Check the various Celiac Societies publications for a suitable product. See page 156 for more details.

Place all the ingredients for the apple stew into a pan. Bring to a simmer, cover, and then turn down the heat, to cook until the apples are soft and pulpy; about 20 minutes. Stir occasionally; you may need to add a little more water if the mixture is too thick. Blend the fruit until smooth, or mash, then cool and chill.

Whisk the cream cheese, yogurt, and condensed milk together until smooth. Stir in the lemon zest and juice, and the mixture will start to thicken. Spoon the mixture into 4–6 small tumblers or glasses. Top the cheesecakes with a layer of the cold apple purée.

Crumble the shortbread and divide the crumbs between the glasses to make the topping. Chill for at least half an hour before serving.

HINTS

- The cheesecake mixture has a strong lemony flavor and can make a fast and easy dessert without the apple.
- The apple stew is delicious served on its own, and is not too sweet. Add a dash of balsamic vinegar and it can be served as an accompaniment to savory food as well.

To store: Keep in the fridge for up to 2 days.
To freeze: Not suitable.

Polenta peach squares

You can use any ripe, fresh fruit instead of the peaches in this cake—cherries in their short season would be wonderful. If frozen peaches are not available, you can substitute canned peaches.

oil, for greasing

1½ sticks unsalted butter

1⅛ cups superfine sugar

3 large eggs, beaten

finely grated zest of 1 large lemon

1 teaspoon vanilla extract

1 tablespoon gluten-free baking powder

1⅔ cups extra fine gluten-free cornmeal (polenta)

2 cups frozen peaches, semi-thawed and drained

confectioners' sugar, for dusting

Preheat the oven to 350°F. Oil an 8-inch square baking pan.

Place the butter and sugar in a mixing bowl and cream them together using a hand-held electric mixer. Add the eggs, half the lemon zest, the vanilla extract, baking powder, and cornmeal, and mix well.

Carefully fold in the drained fruit. Spoon the mixture into the prepared pan, and bake for about 30 minutes until well-risen, golden, and set in the middle. Remove from the oven, and leave to cool a little in the pan.

Transfer to a wire rack to cool completely. Dust with sifted confectioners' sugar and sprinkle with the reserved lemon zest. Cut into 12–16 squares (depending on the size you want) and serve.

To store: Store in an airtight container for up to 3 days.
To freeze: Not suitable.

Frozen fruit pops

Frozen desserts can help soothe sore gums when babies are teething. These fruity treats are popular with older children too!

12 oz frozen fruits, such as Black
   Forest mix or red berries
1 scant cup Greek yogurt
scant ¼ cup confectioners' sugar

Put the frozen fruit, yogurt and confectioners' sugar into a food processor and pulse to blend to the required texture.

Transfer to ice pop molds if you have them, otherwise to ice-cube trays or an airtight container, and freeze until solid. Allow to thaw a little before serving.

HINTS

- If you don't have ice pop molds or ice-cube trays, scoop out little portions from the container to serve.
- For other frozen fruity desserts, any of the fruit purées on page 32 can be frozen in ice pop molds, ice-cube trays, or an airtight container.

Everyday Meals

This chapter covers most areas of cooking, from simple pasta dishes to braises with dumplings. Here I have tried to get a balance of fish, meats, and vegetables, and make the recipes inspiring and packed full of flavor. I like rice, pasta, and potato dishes rather than meals that rely too much on protein, but I've included some hearty dishes, such as Creamy Fish and Corn Chowder (page 62), Chicken Casserole (page 68), and Succulent Pork with Plums (page 72). There are also some sweet offerings, including Orchard Fruit and Almond Crumble (page 85). As in earlier chapters, all the recipes are very simple to cook, and the ingredients are easy to find. Many of the dishes will also freeze well: perfect for the whole family.

Mediterranean roasted vegetable pasta

Roasting vegetables concentrates their natural sweetness and they are full of flavor without the need for salt. Vary the vegetables according to what's in season—you'll need about 1¼ lb prepared weight of mixed vegetables in total.

1 yellow or orange pepper, seeded and chopped into 2-inch chunks

1 red pepper, seeded and chopped into 2-inch chunks

2 medium zucchini, chopped into 2-inch chunks

3 tablespoons olive oil

sprig of fresh thyme or ½ teaspoon dried thyme

2 garlic cloves, whole and unpeeled

2½ cups gluten-free pasta shapes

chopped or grated Pecorino cheese, optional, to serve

FOR THE TOMATO SAUCE

1 tablespoon vegetable oil

1 large red onion, chopped

14-oz can chopped tomatoes

3 salt-free sun-dried tomatoes, chopped

½ teaspoon dried red pepper flakes, optional

1 teaspoon balsamic vinegar

1 teaspoon soft brown sugar

freshly ground black pepper

Preheat the oven to 400°F.

Mix the peppers and zucchini with the oil and thyme and spread out onto a large baking sheet. Tuck in the whole unpeeled cloves of garlic, and then roast for about 40 minutes, until beginning to color. Turn the vegetables over halfway through.

Remove the baking sheet from the oven, squeeze the roasted garlic from the skins, chop, and mix back into the roasted vegetables.

Meanwhile, to make the tomato sauce: heat the vegetable oil in a large pan, and sauté the onion for about 5 minutes. Stir in the remaining ingredients and season well with freshly ground black pepper. Cover and leave to simmer and reduce for about 15–20 minutes. Add the roasted vegetables to the sauce for the last 5 minutes.

Cook the pasta according to the package instructions and drain. Now serve the pasta how you like it: add the cooked pasta to the sauce and stir in small chunks of cheese, if using, or spoon the sauce onto individual portions of the pasta separately, and sprinkle with grated cheese.

HINT
- The sauce is delicious served with polenta (cornmeal) instead of pasta.

To store: Keep the sauce in the fridge for up to 2 days, reheat thoroughly, and serve with freshly cooked pasta.

To freeze: Cool the sauce and freeze in an airtight container. Defrost completely before reheating thoroughly, and serve with freshly cooked pasta.

Warm smoked mackerel with roast carrot wedges and horseradish mayo

I love all smoked fish, though eels are my particular favorite. There are two types of smoked fish—hot- and cold-smoked. Cold-smoked fish, such as smoked salmon, are just warmed in a low smoke to take on the flavor. Mackerel are actually cooked in a hot smoke.

6 medium carrots

4–5 tablespoons olive oil

salt and freshly ground black pepper

4–6 tablespoons good-quality gluten-free mayonnaise

2–3 teaspoons gluten-free creamed horseradish

2 tablespoons chopped fresh mint

2 tablespoons chopped fresh chives

4 small smoked mackerel fillets, at room temperature

green salad, to serve

Preheat the oven to 375°F.

Halve the carrots lengthwise, then cut each half into 4 long wedges. Heat 2 tablespoons of the oil in an ovenproof (preferably a griddle) pan until it just begins to smoke, add the carrot wedges and season well. Transfer the pan to the oven and bake for about 6–8 minutes, then carefully turn the carrots over and carry on baking for another 4–5 minutes.

Meanwhile, mix together the mayonnaise and horseradish and leave to stand so that the flavors infuse.

Place the mint, chives, and 2 tablespoons of the oil in a small blender and blitz to make a smooth paste—you may need to add a dash more oil. Season well with pepper.

Take the cooked carrots out of the oven, pour the herb oil over the top, then turn the carrots to coat well.

Skin the mackerel, and flake the fish into large pieces. To serve, divide the carrots between 4 plates, top with a few flakes of fish, and spoon over some of the mayo. Serve with a green salad.

To store: This is best eaten immediately.
To freeze: Not suitable.

Spiced potato and mint stew

Sometimes a dish comes from nowhere and this is a good example. Leftover cooked spuds and a little spice, mixed with fresh mint and yogurt make a great snack for adults, but the dish is also good for introducing toddlers to mild spices and textures—process the stew slightly or chop the vegetables very small.

SERVES: 4
PREPARATION: 15 MINUTES
COOKING: 15–20 MINUTES

2 tablespoons olive oil
1 teaspoon ground cumin
1 teaspoon ground turmeric
1 teaspoon paprika
2 onions, finely chopped
2 garlic cloves, crushed
12 boiled or roast potatoes, cubed
freshly ground black pepper
2 large tomatoes, roughly chopped
2 tablespoons chopped fresh mint
6 tablespoons natural yogurt,
  to serve

Heat the oil in a medium-sized frying pan or wok. Add half the spices and half the onions and garlic, and cook for 2–3 minutes.

Add half the potatoes, and mix well. Season well with pepper. Cover with a lid, turn down the heat, and cook for 4–5 minutes. Remove this first batch into a bowl and keep warm.

Repeat the process with the other half of the ingredients, then add the first cooked batch. Heat until piping hot. Stir in the tomatoes and chopped mint. Top with the yogurt to serve.

To store: Make as above, but omit the yogurt. Keep in the fridge for up to 2 days and reheat thoroughly before serving with a dollop of yogurt.

To freeze: Make as above, but omit the yogurt. Cool and freeze in an airtight container. Defrost completely before reheating thoroughly, and serve with yogurt.

Twice-cooked cheese and bacon jackets

I just love these; in fact, I like any twice-cooked potato. My mom would cook these for us when we were kids. If you prefer, try using lower-salt ham.

SERVES: 4
PREPARATION: 15 MINUTES
COOKING: 1 HOUR 15 MINUTES

4 large baking potatoes
1 tablespoon vegetable oil
4 bacon strips, chopped
1 large onion, chopped
9 oz mozzarella cheese
freshly ground black pepper

Preheat the oven to 425°F. Prick the potatoes all over and bake in the oven for about 1 hour. Meanwhile, heat the oil in a nonstick frying pan, add the bacon and onion and cook for 15 minutes. Drain and place in a large bowl. Remove the potatoes from the oven when the skins are crisp and the flesh is tender. Cut the potatoes in half lengthwise and set aside to cool a little. Scoop out the cooked potato from the skins and add to the bowl. Stir in the mozzarella and a little pepper and mix lightly. Spoon the potato mixture back into the skins, place on a baking sheet, and pop into the oven for 10–15 minutes.

To store: Bake and fill the potatoes as above, but do not return to the oven once filled. Cool completely, place in an airtight container, and keep in the fridge for up to 2 days, then finish cooking as above, allowing extra time to cook the chilled potatoes.

To freeze: Bake and fill the potatoes as above, but do not return to the oven once filled. Cool and freeze in an airtight container. Defrost, then cook as above, allowing extra time to cook the chilled potatoes.

SERVES: 2–4
PREPARATION: 15 MINUTES
COOKING: 25 MINUTES

Roasted chickpea, tomato, pepper, and Taleggio pasta

Taleggio cheese really adds a kick to this dish; its powerful flavor means a little goes a long way.

14-oz can chickpeas, drained

3 tablespoons olive oil

2 pinches of salt

2 pinches of freshly ground black pepper

4 tablespoons extra-virgin olive oil

2 tablespoons sun-dried tomato paste

1 onion, finely chopped

2 garlic cloves, crushed

3 cups gluten-free fusilli pasta

7 oz roasted peppers from a jar, sliced

4 medium-sized ripe tomatoes, sliced

½ small radicchio lettuce, very finely sliced

2 tablespoons balsamic vinegar

¾ cup Taleggio cheese, cut into ½-inch or slightly smaller cubes

Preheat the oven to 400°F.

Mix the chickpeas with the olive oil, and season with the salt and pepper, place them on a small baking sheet and cook in the oven for 20 minutes, or until slightly browned and dried nicely, but with a soft edge.

Meanwhile, place the extra-virgin olive oil, tomato paste, onion, and garlic in a small pan and cook gently until the onion is soft.

Cook the pasta according to the package instructions. Drain.

Place the sliced peppers and tomatoes in a large bowl, add the warm pasta, and mix well. Add the cooked chickpeas, softened onions and garlic, the lettuce, and vinegar to the pasta bowl, and mix well.

Finally, add the cheese, stir gently, and serve immediately.

HINT

- Any strong cheese will work here, such as a ripe Gorgonzola or Stilton.

To store: This is best eaten immediately.

To freeze: Not suitable.

Creamy fish and corn chowder

I love chowder, especially in this form. The sweetness of the corn and the texture of the fish work really well. Omit the fish and bacon for a good vegetarian version.

1 tablespoon olive oil

1 slice smoked bacon, finely chopped (see Hints, right)

1 leek, finely sliced

1 celery stalk, finely sliced

1 garlic clove, chopped

1 medium potato, cut into small dice

7-oz can corn kernels, drained

3 cups gluten-free vegetable stock (use a gluten-free, reduced-salt vegetable bouillon cube or homemade stock, page 18)

7 oz skinless, boneless white fish, cut into chunks

10 medium cooked and shelled shrimp (see Hints, right)

4 tablespoons heavy cream

1 tablespoon chopped fresh parsley, optional

squeeze of lemon juice

freshly ground black pepper

Heat the oil in a large pan and cook the bacon until golden, about 5 minutes. Add the leek, celery, garlic, and potato. Partially cover the pan and cook gently for 10 minutes, stirring occasionally.

Add the corn kernels and stock and bring back to a simmer, partially cover, and cook for 15 minutes. At this stage, you can thicken the chowder (or skip to the next stage): transfer half to a blender, process and then return it to the pan.

Add the fish and shrimp, and continue to simmer for 5–10 minutes, or until the fish is just cooked through. Remove from the heat, stir in the cream, parsley, lemon juice, and black pepper.

HINTS

- For younger children, it is best to be cautious when introducing fish and shellfish. If you prefer, leave out the shrimp, and substitute them with another white fish such as haddock. Similarly, omit the bacon as it can be salty.
- For adults, a chopped, seeded red chili pepper is an optional garnish.

To store: Best served immediately.

To freeze: Not suitable.

SERVES: 4–6
PREPARATION: 15 MINUTES
COOKING: 50–55 MINUTES

Crunchy salmon and cilantro bake

The simplicity of this dish adds to its allure. Just combine the ingredients, and pop it in the oven—it works really well. And if you have leftover cooked carrots and green beans, it's even quicker to prepare! The secret is to not let the salmon overcook—it should be just cooked through. Other fish will also work well: try mackerel, tuna, pollock, or cod.

2 medium carrots, sliced

¾ cup fine green beans, cut into ¾-inch lengths

18 oz skinless, boneless salmon fillet, cut into ¾-inch cubes

7 oz gluten-free cream cheese*

2 tablespoons milk

3 tablespoons chopped fresh cilantro

salt and freshly ground black pepper

5 slices gluten-free bread*, crusts removed, cut into very small cubes

⅔ cup olive oil

1⅛ cups Cheddar cheese, grated

green salad, to serve

* Check the various Celiac Societies publications for a suitable product. See page 156 for more details.

Preheat the oven to 400°F.

Cook the carrots in a pan of boiling water for 10 minutes. Add the beans to the pan, and cook for another 5 minutes. Drain.

Place the cubed fish, cooked carrots, and beans into a large bowl.

In a separate bowl, mix the cream cheese, milk, cilantro, and seasoning together. Add to the salmon and vegetables, and mix well.

Spoon the mixture into a 12×2-inch-deep baking dish. Toss the gluten-free bread cubes with the olive oil, a little pepper, and the grated cheese, and arrange over the fish mixture. Bake in the oven for 35–40 minutes.

Serve with green salad.

To store: Keep in the fridge for up to 2 days and reheat thoroughly before serving.

To freeze: Cool and freeze in the baking dish. Defrost completely before reheating thoroughly.

Crispy chicken dippers

Always popular with children, but usually covered in bread crumbs. This version is made with a polenta coating for a great, gluten-free crispy crunch.

⅔ cup coarse gluten-free cornmeal (polenta)

1 garlic clove, crushed, optional

freshly ground black pepper

pinch of paprika, optional

1 egg, beaten

3 skinless, boneless chicken breasts, cut into strips

gluten-free tomato ketchup and gluten-free mayonnaise, or Tomato Sauce (see page 40), to serve

Preheat the oven to 400°F. Line a baking sheet with aluminum foil.

Put the cornmeal, garlic, black pepper, and paprika, if using, into a shallow dish or on a plate. Put the egg into a separate dish.

Dip the chicken pieces into the egg, and then roll them in the cornmeal until well coated. Transfer to the lined baking sheet and bake for 20 minutes, or until the chicken is cooked through and golden.

Mix equal quantities of tomato ketchup and mayonnaise to serve as a dip, or serve with homemade Tomato Sauce.

HINTS

- Mix 1 tablespoon grated fresh Parmesan cheese in with the cornmeal for a cheesy coating.
- Use any spices you fancy in the cornmeal coating.
- You could cut the chicken into bite-sized pieces to make chicken nuggets instead of fingers. Bake the nuggets in the oven for 15 minutes, or until the chicken is cooked through and golden.

To store: These are best served immediately.

To freeze: Not suitable.

Chicken casserole

This is a version of the French classic *coq au vin*, though of course without the wine so that all the family can enjoy its delicious full-bodied goodness. It's a bit of work, but well worth the effort for a special occasion meal.

scant ½ stick unsalted butter

4 dry-cured bacon strips, or pancetta slices, cut into ¾-inch cubes

12 shallots, peeled, root left on (so they don't fall apart)

12 button mushrooms

4 chicken legs, halved, knuckles and ball sockets removed, skin on

2 garlic cloves, finely crushed

2 medium carrots, cut into small cubes

2 cups homemade chicken stock

1 tablespoon tomato paste

3 tablespoons roughly chopped fresh tarragon

freshly ground black pepper

2 tablespoons cornstarch or 1 tablespoon arrowroot, optional

4 tablespoons chopped fresh parsley, to garnish

sautéed potatoes, to serve

Preheat the oven to 350°F.

Melt one-quarter of the butter in a large flameproof casserole. Add the bacon and shallots and brown well, probably about 5–6 minutes. Lift out the bacon and shallots and place onto a plate.

Add the mushrooms to the pan and cook until golden brown, then remove and add to the shallots and bacon.

Add the rest of the butter to the pan and heat again. Add the chicken pieces, and brown really well on all sides.

Return the mushrooms, bacon, and shallots to the pan with the garlic and carrots. Pour in the stock, tomato paste, tarragon, and ½ cup water, and season with pepper. Bring to a boil, cover, and cook in the oven for about 45 minutes, or until nicely cooked and colored.

At this point you can thicken the casserole a little with the cornstarch or arrowroot mixed with 2 tablespoons water if needed—entirely optional, though. Remove the chicken pieces from the casserole, and bring it back to a boil on the stovetop, then stir in a little of the cornstarch paste at a time, until you have a thickened sauce. Return the chicken to the casserole.

Garnish with plenty of chopped parsley, and serve with sautéed potatoes.

To store: Keep in the fridge for up to 2 days and reheat thoroughly before serving.

To freeze: Cool and freeze in an airtight container. Defrost completely before reheating thoroughly.

SERVES: 4
PREPARATION: 20 MINUTES
PLUS 30 MINUTES MARINATING
COOKING: 10 MINUTES

Chicken schnitzel burgers with avocado and lime salsa, and sweet pickled onion

This is a brilliantly versatile dish. The same bread crumb coating process works with all meats, even very lean ones that can be notoriously dry, such as pork loin or venison steaks. The coating seals in the moisture, making the meat juicy and flavorful.

1 red onion, very finely sliced into rings

4 tablespoons cider vinegar

pinch of sugar

4 skinless, boneless chicken thighs

4 tablespoons cornstarch or 2 tablespoons arrowroot

1 egg, beaten

10–12 tablespoons gluten-free dried bread crumbs

2 tablespoons oil

2 tablespoons unsalted butter

1 ripe avocado

juice of 1 large lime

½ tablespoon mango chutney

4 tablespoons gluten-free mayonnaise

freshly ground black pepper

TO SERVE

4 gluten-free burger buns, halved

chopped iceberg lettuce

Place the onion slices in a bowl. Add the vinegar, sugar, and plenty of black pepper, mix well, and leave for 30 minutes or longer.

Place a chicken thigh on a large piece of plastic wrap, sprinkle with water, and cover with more plastic wrap. Beat the chicken with a wooden rolling pin or meat mallet until it is nice and thin. Repeat for the remaining 3 thighs.

Put the cornstarch or arrowroot, egg, and bread crumbs onto 3 separate shallow plates. Coat each flattened chicken thigh in a little cornstarch or arrowroot, then in egg, and finally in bread crumbs; pat well.

Heat the oil and butter in a large nonstick frying pan, and fry the crumbed chicken until cooked through, and nicely browned for 10 minutes, turning once.

Meanwhile, peel, pit, and chop the avocado and place in a bowl. Add the lime juice, mango chutney, and mayonnaise, and mix well.

Place the chicken in the split buns, and add a little lettuce. Top with a spoonful of avocado mixture, and then with a few well-drained, pickled onion rings.

To store: Not suitable.
To freeze: Not suitable.

Chicken pot roast with cider and apples

This makes a nice change from the traditional Sunday roast. Serve with mashed potatoes and any green vegetables.

1 tablespoon oil

1 tablespoon unsalted butter

2¾–3¼ lb whole chicken

4 medium eating apples, pared, cored, and thickly sliced

2 onions, sliced

1 fat garlic clove, chopped

1½ cups hard cider or apple cider

¼ teaspoon gluten-free mustard powder

2 teaspoons cornstarch

½ cup heavy cream or half-fat crème fraîche

Preheat the oven to 350°F.

Heat the oil and butter in a large frying pan, and brown the whole chicken on all sides. Transfer the bird to a deep casserole. Tuck the apple slices around the chicken.

Put the onions into the frying pan, and cook until beginning to color. Add the chopped garlic, and fry for a couple of minutes more. Add the cider, mustard, and ½ cup water, and simmer for 5 minutes.

Pour the cider mixture over the chicken and apples. Cover with a lid, and cook in the oven for 1 hour and 15 minutes.

Take the chicken out, divide into portions, and keep warm. For the sauce, mix the cornstarch to a paste with a little of the cooking liquid; add to the pot, and stir in the cream. Bring back to a simmer until thickened. Serve the chicken with the creamy juices.

HINTS

- The chicken can be cooked in a slow cooker for about 3 hours. When the bird is cooked, transfer the cooking liquid to a pan and thicken as above with a cornstarch paste before adding the cream.
- The cooked chicken is soft enough to mash for younger children.

To store: Keep in the fridge for up to 2 days and reheat thoroughly before serving.

To freeze: Cool and freeze in an airtight container. Defrost completely before reheating thoroughly.

Succulent pork with plums

More people have asked me about this recipe than any other over the past year or so. I have even had people contacting me to say they have moved house and lost the recipe and can I resend it! And yes, you do cook the pork in the boiling sugar—it works and it's delicious!

18 oz shoulder of pork, fat on, skinned, and cut into 2½-inch chunks

scant ½ cup sugar

freshly ground black pepper

2 onions, roughly chopped

6 tablespoons gluten-free tamari soy sauce

juice of 1 large lemon

12 ripe plums, halved and pitted

3½ oz gluten-free black pudding, sliced, optional

2¼ cups chicken stock (use a gluten-free, reduced-salt chicken bouillon cube or homemade stock, page 18)

1 tablespoon arrowroot or cornstarch

8 oz frozen peas

boiled new potatoes, to serve

Preheat the oven to 350°F.

Thoroughly dry the pork chunks on paper towels—the drier, the better.

Heat the sugar in a large, heavy-based, flameproof casserole. Stir until you have a thick, not-too-dark caramel; take care here, it's extremely hot.

Season the pork generously with pepper, and then add it to the caramel. Mix well, and cook for 2–3 minutes.

Add the onions, tamari soy sauce, and lemon juice. Bring to a boil, then add the plums and black pudding, if using, and mix well. Add the chicken stock, bring back to a boil, cover, and cook in the oven for 2 hours.

Check to see if the meat is very tender and cooked through. If necessary, thicken the sauce by mixing the arrowroot or cornstarch to a paste with 1 tablespoon cold water, and stirring into the dish. Bring back to a simmer for a couple of minutes.

Finally, stir in the peas, and warm through. Serve with slightly crushed boiled new potatoes.

HINTS

- This is a great recipe for the slow cooker on a low setting for 6–8 hours.
- Use low-salt tamari soy sauce if you can.

To store: Keep in the fridge for up to 2 days and reheat thoroughly before serving.

To freeze: Cool and freeze in an airtight container. Defrost completely before reheating thoroughly.

Velveted pork filet with peppers and garlic

This dish turns pork into a spectacular-tasting, juicy meal. The velveting process (where it is coated in egg white and cornstarch) helps to keep all the moisture in the pork fillet, which has very little fat, making it very healthy indeed. Serve this with rice noodles.

1 large egg white

1 tablespoon cornstarch

1–1¼ lb pork tenderloin or center-cut pork filet, trimmed of any fat or sinew, cut into 8–12 slices

1 red pepper, seeded and cut into strips

1 yellow pepper, seeded and cut into strips

1 medium onion, very finely sliced

4 tablespoons vegetable oil

2 garlic cloves, finely chopped

8 scallions, finely sliced

6 tablespoons gluten-free tamari soy sauce

rice noodles, to serve

Place the egg white and cornstarch in a large bowl and whisk them together briefly. Add the sliced pork and stir to coat.

Place the peppers and onion in a pan, cover with water, and bring to a boil; immediately strain and leave to cool.

Heat a wok or nonstick frying pan with 2 tablespoons of the vegetable oil. Add half the pork and stir-fry until nicely colored. Remove from the wok, and cover with aluminum foil to keep warm. Repeat with the remaining pork.

Wipe the wok with paper towels, add the remaining vegetable oil and heat. Add the cooled peppers and onion, the garlic and scallions, and stir-fry over high heat for 3–4 minutes, or until softened and colored.

Add the pork and any cooking juices and the tamari soy sauce, and stir well until the pork is heated right through. Serve with rice noodles.

To store: This is best eaten immediately.
To freeze: Not suitable.

Fruity pork casserole

This is a very easy dish to prepare and cook; the secret is to not overcook the pork, or it will be stringy and chewy. The golden rule for any cut of pork is: if you cook it slowly, you'll really taste the difference.

1 tablespoon vegetable oil

4 good-sized pork chops,
   skin removed

2 medium onions, finely sliced

¾ cup frozen berries

1 gluten-free, reduced-salt
   chicken bouillon cube

1 tablespoon arrowroot or cornstarch

1 tablespoon cold water

freshly ground black pepper

pinch of soft dark brown sugar to
   taste, optional

mashed or baked potatoes,
   to serve

Heat the oil in a large, deep pan that will hold all the chops. Season the chops with pepper, and brown them, two at a time, in the hot oil on both sides. Once they are browned, lay all four in the bottom of the pan, overlapping slightly.

Sprinkle over the onions, frozen berries, 1 cup water, and the crumbled bouillon cube, and bring to a boil. Then reduce the heat right down to a very gentle simmer. Cover and cook for 40 minutes or so, or until the meat is really soft, but not dry.

Carefully remove the cooked chops from the pan and bring the onions and fruit back to a boil.

Mix the arrowroot or cornstarch to a paste with 1 tablespoon cold water. Drop spoonfuls of paste into the mixture in the pan, until you have a thickened sauce; don't add too much, just enough to thicken nicely. Adjust the seasoning with pepper and a pinch of sugar if necessary.

Return the chops to the pan, cover with the sauce to reheat gently, and serve with mashed or baked potatoes.

To store: Keep in the fridge for up to 2 days, and reheat thoroughly before serving.

To freeze: Cool and freeze in an airtight container. Defrost completely before reheating thoroughly.

Spicy sausage pilaf

Pilaf seems to be a forgotten rice dish, and these days risotto seems to be much more popular. But a pilaf is a great way of cooking rice, and by adding relatively small amounts of other ingredients, you can easily create a one-pot main meal. I like to use spices to help the flavor along, and have suggested a few. However, it's really up to you.

2 tablespoons olive oil

4–6 gluten-free sausages, cut into ½-inch pieces

2 teaspoons cumin seeds

1 teaspoon ground turmeric

2 teaspoons fennel seeds

1 teaspoon finely chopped red chili pepper

½ teaspoon curry powder

2 medium onions, chopped

2 garlic cloves, crushed

2 tablespoons tomato paste

1¼ cups basmati or long-grain rice

½ cup white wine, optional

2½ cups strong chicken stock (use a gluten-free, reduced-salt chicken bouillon cube or homemade stock, page 18)

freshly ground black pepper

4 tablespoons chopped fresh cilantro

Preheat the oven to 375°F.

Heat the oil in a large flameproof casserole, add the sausages and cook for about 5 minutes until they just start to color.

Remove the sausages from the pan, add the spices, chili, and curry powder, and cook for 2 minutes to release their flavors. Add the onions, garlic, and tomato paste, and cook gently for about 5 minutes until softened.

Stir in the rice and coat well in the oils and spices. Add the wine, if using, and stock, and return the sausages to the pan. Season well with pepper, then bring to a boil, stirring.

Cover the casserole with a tight-fitting lid or aluminum foil, and cook in the oven for 14–16 minutes, or until the rice is tender. Remove from the oven, and stir in the fresh cilantro leaves. Cover and leave for another 5 minutes before serving.

To store: This is best eaten immediately.
To freeze: Not suitable.

Spaghetti Bolognese

I got this recipe from an Italian friend and he says it's authentic. There are so many variations that I wasn't really sure, but after some research, this seems to be very close to the traditional recipe. The milk is an optional extra; it just lightens the whole dish, and is quite a popular addition in certain areas of Italy.

2 tablespoons olive oil, plus extra for the pasta

1 small onion, very finely chopped

2 small celery stalks, very finely chopped

1 small carrot, very finely chopped

2 garlic cloves, finely chopped

1 bay leaf, slightly crushed

pinch of dried oregano

1 lb lean ground beef

1 tablespoon tomato paste

1¼ cups tomato sauce

2 large glasses of red wine, Barbera is perfect

freshly ground black pepper

1¼ cups gluten-free strong beef stock

2 tablespoons cornstarch or arrowroot

2–3 tablespoons milk

12 oz gluten-free spaghetti

grated fresh Parmesan cheese, to serve

Heat the olive oil in a large pan and add the onion, celery, carrot, garlic, bay leaf, and oregano and cook for 3 minutes to soften.

Add the ground beef, break it up with a wooden spoon, and cook for about 6–7 minutes until starting to brown. Add the tomato paste, tomato sauce, wine, and plenty of black pepper, and cook over low heat for a few minutes.

Finally, add the stock, partially cover with a lid, and bring to a very slow simmer. Cook for 1 hour, very slowly.

Mix the cornstarch or arrowroot to a paste with 2 tablespoons cold water, and add to the simmering meat sauce, stirring constantly, to thicken it. You should end up with a loose sauce that coats the pasta. Add a touch of milk and keep the sauce warm.

Cook the spaghetti in plenty of boiling water according to the package instructions, drain, and add a touch of oil to prevent it sticking.

Divide the pasta between 4–6 plates, top with some sauce, and serve with grated Parmesan cheese.

To store: Keep the sauce in the fridge for up to 2 days, reheat thoroughly, and serve with freshly cooked pasta.

To freeze: Cool the sauce and freeze in an airtight container. Defrost completely before reheating thoroughly and serving with freshly cooked pasta.

Braised beef with spices and mashed potato topping

One of the best things about autumn is that it's a great time to enjoy a hearty stew. Here's one with a twist. Topped with a delicious layer of thick mashed potatoes, this will keep in the fridge for a few days, and will freeze well. It's a good idea to make a double batch, and place one in the freezer.

2 tablespoons vegetable oil

12 oz chuck steak, cut into 1-inch cubes

½ tablespoon tomato paste

1 tablespoon gluten-free creamed or fresh horseradish

2 teaspoons sugar

1 small red onion, chopped

1 red pepper, chopped into large pieces

¼ teaspoon chili powder

4 oz mushrooms, quartered

1 gluten-free beef bouillon cube

salt and freshly ground black pepper

2 cups (about 1 lb) warm, buttery mashed potatoes with black pepper

Preheat the oven to 350°F.

Heat 1 tablespoon of the oil in an ovenproof casserole, then add the meat and cook until browned all over. Add the tomato paste, horseradish, and sugar, and set aside.

Heat the remaining tablespoon of oil in a frying pan. Add the onion, pepper, and chili powder, and cook gently until the vegetables are softened and golden brown.

Tip the mixture into the casserole dish with the beef and stir together. Next add the mushrooms.

Add enough boiling water to barely cover the meat and vegetables (about 1¼ cups) and crumble in the bouillon cube. Season well with salt and black pepper.

Cover the casserole with a tight-fitting lid, place in the oven and cook for 2 hours, nice and gently. The meat should become juicy and tender, and should fall apart when gently squeezed.

Transfer to a clean baking dish. Cover with a thick layer of the mashed potatoes, and place back in the oven to brown slightly, for 15–20 minutes.

Serve each portion of beef and mashed potato with a little steamed broccoli, green beans, or snow peas.

To store: Keep in the fridge for up to 3 days and reheat thoroughly before serving.

To freeze: Cool and freeze in an airtight container. Defrost completely before reheating thoroughly.

Braised lamb with parsley and mint dumplings

Many people have written and emailed me, asking about gluten-free dumplings. Well, here you go! It took a bit of time to research, but I'm happy with this version.

FOR THE LAMB

2–3 tablespoons olive oil

18 oz shoulder of lamb, cut into 1½-inch cubes

3–4 tablespoons Gluten-free Flour Mix A (see page 19)

1 tablespoon tomato paste

2 small onions, roughly chopped

2 medium carrots, roughly chopped

2 large potatoes, cut into ¾-inch cubes

1 gluten-free, reduced-salt chicken or beef bouillon cube

½ teaspoon freshly ground black pepper

mashed potatoes and peas, to serve

FOR THE DUMPLINGS

scant ¾ cup Gluten-free Flour Mix A (see page 19), plus extra for hands

1 teaspoon gluten-free baking powder

3½ tablespoons gluten-free beef suet or shortening

2 tablespoons chopped fresh parsley

2 tablespoons chopped fresh mint

salt and freshly ground black pepper

Preheat the oven to 350°F.

Heat the oil in an ovenproof (10-inch x 4¾-inch-deep) casserole. Coat the lamb in the flour, and add to the pan in small batches. Brown the meat really well, and keep the pan fairly hot. Remove each batch of browned meat to make way for the next, and then return it all to the pan with any juices.

Turn the heat down, add the tomato paste, and mix well to coat. Next add the prepared vegetables, stir well, add 2 cups boiling water and crumble in the bouillon cube. Add the pepper, and bring back to a simmer. Cover the casserole and cook in the oven for 1 hour.

Meanwhile, make the dumplings by mixing all the dry ingredients together and then adding enough cold water to make a firm dough (about 3–3½ fl oz). The mix will be slightly sticky. Divide the dough into 8 equal pieces. Flour your hands well, and roll each piece into a loose ball.

At the 1 hour mark, carefully remove the lid from the casserole and add the dumplings. Return to the oven, uncovered, for about 40–50 minutes, or until the dumplings are well browned and puffed up. Serve with mashed potatoes and peas.

To store: Cook the lamb in the oven for 1 hour as above (without the dumplings), then cool and keep in the fridge for up to 2 days. Make the dumplings fresh, as above, pop them into the casserole and cook at 350°F for 50–60 minutes.

To freeze: Cook the lamb in the oven for 1 hour as above (without the dumplings), then cool and freeze in an airtight container. Defrost completely. Make the dumplings fresh, as above, pop them into the casserole and cook at 350°F for 50–60 minutes.

Baked fruit

This works well with any single pitted fruit in season or a combination, such as nectarines, plums, peaches, and apricots.

5 pitted fruit of your choice (see introduction), quartered and pits removed
juice of 1 small orange

Preheat the oven to 400°F.

Place the fruit on a large square of thick aluminum foil and pull up the sides to make an open package. Squeeze the orange juice over the fruit, and then loosely seal the fruit in the foil. Bake the package for 10–15 minutes, until the fruit is just soft.

HINT

- To make a nice crunchy topping to contrast with the soft fruit, sprinkle gluten-free muesli or cereal on top of the cooked fruit just before serving.

To store: Keep in the fridge for up to 2 days and serve cold or reheat thoroughly before serving hot.

To freeze: Cool and freeze in an airtight container. Defrost completely before serving cold or reheating thoroughly to serve hot.

Raspberry yogurt smoothie

Smoothies are all the rage now. They're a great way of adding fruit to any diet without too much extra sugar and fat.

heaping ½ cup plain yogurt

1 small banana

1 cup frozen raspberries

½ cup fruit juice, such as pressed apple or diluted cranberry juice

1–2 teaspoons clear honey or confectioners' sugar, to sweeten, optional

Place the yogurt, fruit, and juice in a blender and blitz until smooth. Add more juice or water if needed to adjust to the required thickness. Taste and sweeten with honey or confectioners' sugar if necessary. Serve immediately.

HINTS

- Frozen blueberries, or a combination of ripe peaches and nectarines also work well.
- This recipe is not recommended for younger babies because it contains honey, which can cause a rare form of food poisoning in babies under 1 year.

To store: This is best served immediately.

To freeze: Not suitable.

Orchard fruit and almond crumble

The rule to remember with crumble is to add the sugar after the butter is rubbed into the flour. Then just scatter it over the fruit; do not pack it down but leave it as light and fluffy as possible.

26 oz mixed fruit, such as apples, plums, raspberries, and peaches

2 tablespoons superfine sugar

1 tablespoon apple juice or water

FOR THE CRUMBLE TOPPING

scant ¾ cup Gluten-free Flour Mix A (see page 19)

scant ½ cup ground almonds

scant ¾ stick unsalted butter, chilled

6 tablespoons turbinado sugar

6 small amaretti cookies, crushed

1 tablespoon flaked almonds

Preheat the oven to 400°F.

Pare and core the apples and cut into thin slices. Quarter and pit the plums and pit and slice the peaches. Place the fruit into a shallow baking dish, sprinkle with the sugar and juice or water.

To make the crumble topping, place the flour, almonds and butter into a food processor and pulse just until the mixture looks like coarse bread crumbs. Transfer to a bowl and gently stir in the sugar.

Spoon the crumble over the top of the fruit. Sprinkle with the crushed amaretti cookies and flaked almonds.

Bake in the preheated oven for about 35 minutes until the top is golden, and the juices are bubbling.

To store: Keep in the fridge for up to 2 days and reheat thoroughly before serving.

To freeze: Cool and freeze the crumble in the baking dish. Defrost completely and reheat thoroughly before serving.

Cooking on Their Own

The recipes for this chapter came about for two reasons. First, my plumber's teenage lad is a celiac. He lives at home and his mom makes his packed lunch every day. We got to chatting one day and he said that at some point soon he would be leaving home. I asked if he could cook, to which he replied, "No." He was quite concerned about having to cook on his own. Second, one of my stepson's friends is a celiac who will be going off to university next year. He was also worried. This section covers simple, relatively inexpensive food that I reckon almost anybody can cook, from Thai Green Chicken Curry (page 92) to Lasagna (page 95), to Beef Chili (page 96).

Mushy pea cakes with sweet soft onions

A great dish for a filling meal, really tasty and so cheap too—I absoutely love it! I once cooked these pea cakes on a TV program and got a great response.

FOR THE SAUCE

10-oz can petit pois, drained and mashed

2 tablespoons olive oil

pinch of gluten-free, reduced-salt vegetable bouillon cube

dash of vinegar

salt and freshly ground black pepper

1 tablespoon olive oil

1 onion, thinly slived

FOR THE PEA CAKES

10-oz can mushy peas* or canned petit pois, drained and mashed

4 tablespoons gluten-free dried bread crumbs

½ teaspoon Madras curry powder

½ teaspoon ground cumin

½ small onion, finely chopped

1 garlic clove, crushed

dash of vinegar

4 tablespoons cornstarch or arrowroot

olive oil, for frying

Place all the ingredients for the sauce into a small pan and bring to a boil, then keep warm.

Meanwhile, heat the oil in a frying pan and cook the onion rings over a medium heat until browned and a little crispy. Keep warm.

To make the cakes, place the peas, bread crumbs, curry powder, cumin, chopped onion, garlic, and vinegar in a mixing bowl and stir really well to combine.

Divide the pea cake mixture into 8 small balls, about the size of a walnut, then flatten slightly. Dust the patties in the cornstarch or arrowroot.

Heat some olive oil in a large nonstick frying pan. Fry the cakes for 3–4 minutes on each side, then place on paper towels to drain.

Place a little sauce on 4 warm plates, top with a warm onion slice and finally top with a couple of patties. Serve any remaining sauce separately.

To store: Keep the uncooked patties in the fridge for up to 2 days, and cook as above before serving. Keep the sauce in the fridge for up to 2 days, and reheat thoroughly before serving.

To freeze: Cool the uncooked patties and the sauce, and freeze in separate airtight containers. Defrost the patties and sauce completely. Cook the patties as above, and reheat the sauce thoroughly before serving.

*This very British ingredient can either be bought canned on the internet, or you can buy dried marrowfat peas, soak them overnight and then boil them down, or use ordinary canned peas and mash them.

Quick egg-fried rice with cannellini beans

SERVES: 2
PREPARATION: 10 MINUTES
COOKING: 20 MINUTES

A speedy recipe that is easy to shop for and cook. The basic egg-fried rice can be used as the starting point for other dishes too—a little chopped, cooked meat or shrimp, for instance, will make a really tasty meal.

4 tablespoons vegetable oil
2 large eggs, beaten
1 small onion, finely chopped
2 garlic cloves, finely chopped
15½-oz can cannellini beans, drained and well rinsed
1¼ cups cooked gluten-free basmati rice
freshly ground black pepper

Heat half the oil in a wok or large frying pan, add the beaten eggs, and cook until very dry. Remove from the wok, and keep warm.

Add the rest of the oil to the wok, add the onion and garlic, and cook for 5 minutes.

Stir in the beans and warm through for another 5 minutes, add the hot rice, and heat through for 5 minutes more until steaming hot.

Return the egg mixture to the pan, and season well with black pepper before serving.

To store: Not suitable.
To freeze: Not suitable.

Thai green chicken curry

Ever since I cooked this on TV, I've had lots of calls about it. It's packed full of flavor and quite straightforward to do.

4 tablespoons vegetable oil

8 skinless, boneless chicken thighs, cut into ¾-inch pieces

2 teaspoons cornstarch

2 tablespoons shallots, finely chopped

2 tablespoons finely chopped fresh ginger root

3 garlic cloves, crushed

1–2 tablespoons gluten-free Thai fish sauce

2 teaspoons tamarind paste

4 teaspoons gluten-free Thai green curry paste

dash of gluten-free tamari soy sauce

½ cup strong gluten-free chicken stock (use a gluten-free, reduced-salt chicken bouillon cube or homemade stock, page 18)

2 teaspoons sugar

1½ cups coconut milk

juice of 3 limes

6 tablespoons chopped fresh basil leaves

2 tablespoons chopped fresh cilantro

steamed rice, to serve

Heat the vegetable oil in a wok or deep frying pan. Stir the chicken pieces and cornstarch together. Add the chicken pieces to the wok, and stir-fry until they have taken on a little color, then put into a colander, placed over a bowl, to drain.

Pour some of the drained oil back into the wok and reheat. Add the shallots, ginger, and garlic and cook for 3 minutes.

Add the Thai fish sauce, tamarind and curry pastes, tamari soy sauce, chicken stock, sugar, coconut milk, and lime juice and cook for 3 minutes more.

Return the chicken to the wok and simmer for another 10 minutes, until cooked through.

Finally stir in the basil and cilantro, and check the seasoning. Serve with steamed rice.

To store: Keep in the fridge for up to 2 days and reheat thoroughly before serving.

To freeze: Cool and freeze in an airtight container. Defrost completely before reheating thoroughly.

Chicken fajitas

Another dish that's all the rage at the moment. The key to its success are the various textures and flavor combination of the ingredients: avocado, tomatoes, onions, corn, and peppers. This dish makes a lovely supper or lunch.

FOR THE SALSA

2 ripe tomatoes

1 small avocado

2 scallions

3 tablespoons canned corn kernels, drained

1–2 teaspoons lemon juice

FOR THE FAJITAS

1 tablespoon canola or olive oil

1 small onion, sliced into strips

1 yellow or orange pepper, seeded and sliced into strips

2 skinless, boneless chicken breasts, sliced into strips

pinch of mild curry or chili powder, optional

1½ tablespoons mild cheese, grated, optional

2 gluten-free tortilla wraps (see Hints, right)

Preheat the oven to 400°F.

To make the salsa, finely chop the tomato, avocado, and scallions, and mix together with the corn and lemon juice. Set aside to allow the flavors to develop.

For the fajitas, heat the oil in a frying pan, add the onion, pepper, chicken, and curry or chili powder, and sauté until the chicken is cooked through, approximately 8–10 minutes.

Meanwhile, wrap the tortillas in aluminum foil and place in the oven for about 5 minutes until soft and piping hot. Divide the hot chicken fajita mix between the tortillas, and spoon over a little salsa. Sprinkle with some grated cheese, if using, roll up each tortilla and cut in half. Serve any remaining salsa on the side.

HINTS

- This is a versatile recipe which can be made with beef strips, tofu, or mashed beans instead of the chicken. For bean fajitas, use canned borlotti or mixed beans, drain, rinse, mash well, and then heat with 1 teaspoon spice such as ras el hanout, a blend of ground Moroccan spices.
- If gluten-free tortilla wraps are hard to find, use gluten-free pita breads instead.

To store: Not suitable.

To freeze: Not suitable.

Lasagna

SERVES: 6
PREPARATION: 20 MINUTES
COOKING: 1 HOUR 20 MINUTES –
1 HOUR 40 MINUTES

No book like this would be complete without a lasagna recipe, so here it is. I purposely use small amounts of pasta, otherwise you end up with a pasta cake!

8 gluten-free lasagna sheets, each
   9½ x 2 inches
4 tablespoons grated fresh
   Parmesan cheese
green salad, to serve

FOR THE MEAT SAUCE

4 tablespoons olive oil
1 large onion, finely chopped
4 garlic cloves, chopped
18 oz lean ground beef or vegetarian
   alternative
1 tablespoon cornstarch
⅔ cup red wine or water
14-oz can chopped tomatoes
½ gluten-free, reduced-salt beef
   bouillon cube
1 teaspoon dried oregano
small bunch of fresh basil, chopped
freshly ground black pepper

FOR THE WHITE SAUCE

2 cups milk
2 tablespoons unsalted butter, at
   room temperature
2½ tablespoons cornstarch
pinch of grated nutmeg

To make the meat sauce, heat the oil in a large pan and sauté the onion for 10–15 minutes. Add the garlic, and cook for another 2 minutes. Add the ground beef, and cook until lightly colored, breaking it up well.

Add the cornstarch and stir well, then add the wine or water, tomatoes, crumbled bouillon cube, herbs, and pepper. Bring to a boil, and simmer for 25–30 minutes, stirring occasionally to prevent it from sticking.

Meanwhile, make the white sauce. Gently heat the milk in a small pan, and while it is warming, work the butter and cornstarch together to a paste. Break off small pieces and whisk into the simmering milk: it will thicken almost immediately. Add the nutmeg and black pepper, and stir well. Remove from the heat, and place a layer of plastic wrap over the surface to prevent a skin forming.

Preheat the oven to 350°F.

Spread one-third of the meat sauce over the base of a 2-quart baking dish, approximately 9½ inches square. Place half the lasagna sheets over the sauce. Cover the lasagna with another third of the meat sauce. Add about one-third of the white sauce. Top with the remaining pasta and meat sauce, and finally, pour over the rest of the white sauce. Sprinkle with the cheese, and cover loosely with foil. Bake for 35–45 minutes. Remove the foil for the last 20 minutes.

Remove from the oven and allow to cool slightly before eating with a large green salad.

To store: Keep in the fridge for up to 2 days and reheat thoroughly before serving.
To freeze: Cool and freeze in the baking dish. Defrost completely before reheating thoroughly.

Beef chili

Everyone loves a good chili. I was very lucky some years ago to visit San Antonio, Texas, where I learned many things, but the best of all was how to cook a real chili, and here it is. The American version is much runnier than the European version; it's delicious and can be made with beef, lamb, pork, or venison. I have also cooked a meat-free version using soy protein—very good, again, but you need more liquid with the soy.

1 tablespoon vegetable oil

4 large onions, finely chopped

4 garlic cloves, chopped

18 oz ground beef or 12 oz gluten-free textured vegetable protein

1 tablespoon ground cumin

2 teaspoons ground cinnamon

2 tablespoons paprika, optional

2 teaspoons dried red pepper flakes

freshly ground black pepper

2 tablespoons dried oregano

14-oz can chopped tomatoes

4 tablespoons tomato paste

2 tablespoons sugar

14-oz can black-eyed peas, drained

14-oz can mung or kidney beans, drained

TO SERVE

guacamole

sour cream

gluten-free tortillas or gluten-free pita bread

Heat the oil in a large pan, add the onions and garlic, and cook gently, to soften.

Add the ground meat or textured vegetable protein, and break up well with a wooden spoon. Then cook until all the moisture has evaporated, and the meat is starting to brown nicely.

Next add the spices, oregano, tomatoes, tomato paste, sugar, and 1¾ cups water. Mix well and add the beans. Cook gently for 30-40 minutes, to reduce the liquid and concentrate the flavor. Taste and adjust the seasoning about halfway through.

Serve with guacamole, sour cream, and tortillas, or pita bread.

To store: Keep in the fridge for up to 2 days and reheat thoroughly before serving.

To freeze: Cool and freeze in an airtight container. Defrost completely before reheating thoroughly.

Baked ham with pineapple chutney

This recipe is so easy—just wrap the ham in aluminum foil, pop it in the oven to bake, and then make a simple chutney. I also like to bake some spuds at the same time, saving time and energy.

1½ lb (approximately) unsmoked raw ham

4 medium potatoes, skins on, scrubbed

8-oz can pineapple chunks in juice, drained

1 small red onion

1 small apple, pared and cored

2 tablespoons brown sugar

3 tablespoons malt vinegar

pinch of dried red pepper flakes, optional

2 tablespoons olive oil

freshly ground black pepper

Preheat the oven to 375°F.

Wash the ham really well. Scrunch up a large piece of aluminum foil, sit it on a baking sheet and place the ham on top. Cover the ham with two layers of foil, and wrap well. Bake for 2½–3 hours.

After 1½ hours, place the potatoes in the oven next to the ham.

To make the chutney, finely chop the pineapple, onion, and apple, place into a bowl, and mix really well. Add the sugar, vinegar, red pepper flakes, and olive oil, season with black pepper, and mix well. Cover and leave until needed.

Next, check if the ham is cooked. Remove the baking sheet from the oven, open the foil (take care as the hot steam will rush out), and insert a skewer through the vent. There should be a little resistance, but the meat should not be too firm. A meat thermometer should show an internal temperature of 160°F.

Slice the ham thickly, and serve with the chutney and baked potatoes.

To store: Keep the ham in the fridge for up to 2 days and serve cold.

To freeze: Cool and freeze both the ham and chutney in airtight containers. Defrost completely before reheating thoroughly.

Potato and ham hash with arugula and apple salad

This is a great way to use up any leftover vegetables—a little goes a long way here. I like to use leftover roasted potatoes, but there often aren't any. Luckily boiled potatoes work just as well!

2 large carrots, cut into small chunks

4 medium potatoes, cut into small chunks

½ medium cauliflower, broken into bite-sized florets

5 tablespoons olive oil

1 onion, sliced

1 gluten-free, reduced-salt chicken bouillon cube

7 oz cooked ham, cut into ½-inch cubes

freshly ground black pepper

4 large eggs

FOR THE SALAD

5 oz (about 3 cups) arugula leaves

2 small McIntosh apples, skin on, but cored

2 tablespoons olive oil

squeeze of lemon juice

Place the carrot and potato chunks in a pan of boiling water and cook for 5 minutes. Add the cauliflower florets and cook for another 5 minutes. Drain and set aside.

Heat 4 tablespoons of the oil in a large, nonstick frying pan. Add the onion and cook for a few minutes to brown slightly. Next add the carrots, potatoes, and cauliflower, and continue to cook until they all take on a little color.

Next, add the crumbled bouillon cube, a scant ½ cup cold water, the cubed ham, and a generous dash of pepper. Bring to a boil.

Stir well and cook over low heat, covered with a tight-fitting lid, for 20 minutes. When the vegetables are cooked, check the seasoning, adjust if needed, and keep warm.

Meanwhile, make the salad. Place the arugula into a large bowl, then grate the apple on a coarse grater. Add to the arugula and mix well, but lightly. Add the olive oil and lemon juice, and mix well again, but do not crush the arugula.

In another pan, heat the remaining oil and fry the eggs for 3–4 minutes, until the whites appear solid.

Serve the hash in deep bowls, and top each portion with a fried egg. Serve the salad separately.

To store: Not suitable.
To freeze: Not suitable.

Pork and sesame stir-fry

Pork is the most eaten meat in the world. I think it's partly because you can add any flavor profile to it. Here is an example that combines sweet, sour, spicy, and strong oils, such as sesame.

4 tablespoons gluten-free sweet chili sauce

2 tablespoons clear honey

3 tablespoons rice vinegar or lime juice

1 teaspoon toasted sesame oil

1 teaspoon Chinese five-spice powder

1 tablespoon vegetable oil

14 oz pork loin, sliced into strips

1 lb prepared stir-fry vegetables, such as sliced carrots, sugarsnap peas, broccoli, and scallions

sesame seeds, for sprinkling

Mix the chili sauce with the honey, vinegar, sesame oil, and five-spice powder.

Heat the oil in a large frying pan or wok, and stir-fry the pork strips over high heat until cooked through. Remove from the pan.

Add the vegetables to the pan and stir-fry for 5–10 minutes.

Add the chili sauce mixture to the pan and heat until bubbling. Return the meat to the pan to warm through, then sprinkle with sesame seeds. Serve immediately.

HINTS

- Use strips of chicken or beef filet instead of the pork.
- Try other vegetables such as sliced peppers or baby corn.
- This recipe is not recommended for younger babies because it contains honey and sesame. Honey can cause a rare form of food poisoning in babies under 1 year. Very occasionally babies can have a sesame-seed allergy, but they should be safe from 6 months.

To store: Not suitable.

To freeze: Not suitable.

Tagliatelle with bacon, parsley, red onion, and cherry tomatoes

This idea came to light one night when all we had in the fridge were the ingredients listed above. With a little bit of thought I came up with this great supper dish! The secret is just to warm the tomatoes through.

3 tablespoons olive oil

1 large red onion, chopped

1 garlic clove, crushed

4 rindless smoked Canadian bacon slices, cut into ½-inch strips

8 oz gluten-free tagliatelle

11 oz (about 25) cherry tomatoes, halved

2 tablespoons chopped fresh flat leaf parsley

2–4 tablespoons crème fraîche

salt and freshly ground black pepper

finely grated Parmesan cheese, to serve

Heat 2 tablespoons of the olive oil in a heavy-based pan, add the onion and garlic, and cook gently for about 5–8 minutes, until they are soft, but not colored.

Add the bacon to the pan and cook until crispy; cook it slowly so it doesn't burn.

Cook the tagliatelle in a large pan of boiling water, according to the package instructions, until just tender. Drain the cooked tagliatelle, add a touch of olive oil, and mix well: this will prevent it sticking together.

Add the halved tomatoes to the pan containing the onion and bacon, and warm until they are just beginning to break down, but do not overcook.

Take the pan off the heat, and stir in the parsley and crème fraîche, then season well. You can serve this in two ways—either tip the tagliatelle into the sauce and stir to coat, or spoon the tagliatelle into individual bowls, and pour the sauce over the top. Sprinkle with grated Parmesan.

To store: Not suitable.
To freeze: Not suitable.

Cheesy smoked bacon chili fries

This seems to have become a student staple over the years, and here's my version. I make no apology for it—it's just very tasty convenience food!

SERVES: 4-6
PREPARATION: 10 MINUTES
COOKING: 30 MINUTES

18 oz gluten-free oven fries
6 smoked bacon strips
1 teaspoon dried red pepper flakes
1¾ cups grated extra sharp Cheddar cheese

Preheat the oven to 400°F.

Place the fries onto a large baking sheet and cook in the oven according to the package instructions.

Chop the bacon into thin pieces and place in a frying pan. Heat gently until the fat runs from the bacon, at which point add the red pepper flakes and cook gently.

Once the fries are cooked, remove from the oven. Sprinkle the bacon and chili over, and then smother with the cheese.

Return the fries to the oven and heat until the cheese is just melted. Tuck in…

To store: Not suitable.
To freeze: Not suitable.

Tuna, spinach, and corn pasta bake

Almost everyone I know has cooked a version of this smashing classic dish. Simple and tasty, it's always a success.

SERVES: 4-6
PREPARATION: 15 MINUTES
COOKING: 30 MINUTES

9 oz gluten-free pasta, preferably fusilli
2 cups milk
2 tablespoons unsalted butter, at room temperature
2½ tablespoons cornstarch
pinch of cracked black pepper
1 teaspoon anchovy essence
2 × 7-oz cans tuna, well drained
1⅛ cups sharp Cheddar cheese, roughly grated
1 scant cup spinach leaves
4 tablespoons roughly chopped fresh basil
7-oz can corn kernels, drained
2-3 large tomatoes, sliced

Preheat the oven to 400°F.

Cook the pasta in plenty of boiling water according to the package instructions and drain well.

Gently heat the milk in a small pan, and while it is warming, work the butter and cornstarch together to form a paste. Break off small pieces and whisk into the simmering milk: it will thicken almost immediately. Add the cracked black pepper and anchovy essence, and mix well. Next, stir in the tuna, half the cheese, the spinach, basil, corn, and cooked pasta, and mix everything together.

Spoon into a large baking dish, top with overlapping tomato slices, and finally the rest of the cheese.

Bake for about 15 minutes, until the cheese is nicely browned.

To store: Best served immediately.
To freeze: Not suitable.

Beef and Cheddar cobbler

Another interesting but easy recipe that will produce great results. Ground beef is cheap and this cobbler topping (actually made of biscuits) sets it off perfectly. The dish freezes really well.

2 tablespoons vegetable oil

2 small onions, chopped

1 teaspoon dried oregano, optional

2 garlic cloves, chopped

7 oz mushrooms, thickly sliced

18 oz ground beef

2 × 14-oz cans chopped tomatoes with herbs

2 gluten-free, reduced-salt beef bouillon cubes

2 tablespoons cornstarch or 1 tablespoon arrowroot

freshly ground black pepper

FOR THE COBBLER TOPPING

2½ cups Gluten-free Flour Mix A (see page 19)

¾ stick cooking margarine

pinch of salt

2 teaspoons dried oregano

2 teaspoons xanthan gum

3 teaspoons gluten-free baking powder

2 large eggs, lightly beaten

¾ cup Cheddar cheese, finely grated

½ cup milk, warmed, plus extra for glazing

Heat the vegetable oil in a large pan. Add the chopped onions, oregano, garlic, and mushrooms. Cook over high heat for 10 minutes.

Add the ground beef, break up well, and cook until it changes from red to a light brown color. Stir in the tomatoes, crumble in the bouillon cubes, and mix really well. Simmer gently for 20 minutes.

Mix the cornstarch or arrowroot with 2 tablespoons cold water and add a little of the paste to thicken the sauce slightly—don't go mad. Spoon the beef into a 10-inch square baking dish and set aside to cool slightly while you make the cobbler topping.

Preheat the oven to 400°F.

Place the flour, margarine, salt, oregano, and xanthan gum into a bowl, and rub together with your fingers to form fine bread crumbs. Add the baking powder, eggs, cheese, and warm milk, and mix together to form a dough.

Gently roll the dough out to about 1 inch thick. Using a 1¼-inch plain cutter, cut out 12–14 small, plump biscuits. Brush the biscuits with milk, and arrange over the cooled beef mixture.

Bake the cobbler for 15–20 minutes, or until the biscuits are baked and the beef is heated right through.

To store: Keep in the fridge for up to 2 days and reheat thoroughly before serving.

To freeze: Cool and freeze in the baking dish. Defrost completely before reheating thoroughly.

Triple chocolate rock cakes

My mom always made lovely rock cakes (similar to what Americans would call drop cookies). Here's a modern twist on Mom's classic, updated with chocolate! Perfect.

vegetable oil, for greasing

heaping 1¾ cups Gluten-free Flour Mix A (see page 19)

2 teaspoons gluten-free baking powder

¼ teaspoon baking soda

1 teaspoon xanthan gum

1 stick unsalted butter

scant ½ cup superfine sugar

grated zest of 1 orange

¾ cup juicy golden raisins

1 heaping tablespoon gluten-free milk chocolate, chopped

1 heaping tablepoon gluten-free dark chocolate, chopped

1 heaping tablespoon gluten-free white chocolate, chopped

2 eggs, beaten

Preheat the oven to 400°F. Oil a baking sheet.

Sift the flour, baking powder, baking soda, and xanthan gum into a large bowl. Rub the butter into the flour mixture with your fingers until crumbs just start to form, but do not overwork the mixture.

Stir in the sugar, orange zest, golden raisins, and all the chopped chocolate. Add the eggs and bring the mixture together to form a fairly stiff (but not dry) dough—clean hands are best for this job.

Break off pieces of dough about the size of a walnut and place onto the baking sheet. Bake for 15–20 minutes until set but not overbaked. Remove from the oven and allow to cool a little.

These should be served warm.

To store: Store in an airtight container for up to 2 days. For best results, microwave for a few seconds to warm through before serving.

To freeze: Cool and freeze in an airtight container. Allow to defrost completely, and for best results, microwave for a few seconds to warm through before serving.

Melting-middle cupcakes

Serve these little cakes warm, as a dessert, or just for a treat. The chocolate combination in the center can be with anything you like—try adding orange zest or using gluten-free white chocolate instead of the dark chocolate. The cakes are easy to make: just remember to have all your ingredients at room temperature before you start, measure carefully and bake them as soon as you have made the mixture.

½ cup canola oil

½ cup whole milk

1 teaspoon vanilla extract

1⅓ cups gluten-free all-purpose flour

½ cup cocoa powder

1½ teaspoons gluten-free baking powder

½ teaspoon xanthan gum

heaping ¾ cup superfine sugar

2 large eggs

12 squares of gluten-free dark chocolate

2 tablespoons chocolate hazelnut spread

Preheat the oven to 375°F. Line a muffin pan with 12 paper cupcake cases (not muffin cases, which are larger).

Mix the oil, milk, and vanilla together in a pitcher and set aside.

Sift the flour, cocoa powder, baking powder, and xanthan gum together in a bowl.

Place the superfine sugar and eggs in another bowl, and whisk together using an electric hand mixer on high speed for 2–3 minutes, until the mixture is thick and light, and the beaters leave a trail. Whisk in the oil, and mix on low speed until just combined. Finally evenly incorporate the flour mixture. The batter should be quite soft and wet.

Half-fill the paper cases with the mixture. Place a square of chocolate and ½ teaspoon blob of hazelnut spread in the center of each cup. Spoon the rest of the mixture on top (to about ½ inch from the top) and bake for about 20 minutes until well-risen.

Remove from the oven and cool on a wire rack. Serve warm.

To store: These are best served on the day they are made.
To freeze: Not suitable.

Zingy lemon cupcakes

A nice twist on lemon drizzle cake. These also freeze really well.

½ cup canola oil

½ cup whole milk

1¼ cups Gluten-free Flour Mix A
(see page 19)

1½ teaspoons gluten-free baking
powder

½ teaspoon xanthan gum

grated zest of 1 large lemon

Heaping ¾ cup superfine sugar

2 large eggs

confectioners' sugar, sifted for
dusting

Preheat the oven to 375°F. Line a muffin pan with 12 paper cupcake cases.

Mix the oil and milk together in a pitcher and set aside.

Sift the flour, baking powder, and xanthan gum in a bowl. Mix in the lemon zest.

Place the superfine sugar and eggs in another bowl and whisk on high speed, using an electric hand mixer, for 2–3 minutes.

Once the egg and sugar mixture is thick enough to leave a trail when the beaters are lifted out of the mixture, add the flour and oil mixtures and fold in thoroughly. The resulting batter should be quite soft and wet.

Fill the paper cases to about ½ inch from the top and bake for 15–20 minutes until well-risen and golden.

Remove from the oven and cool on a wire rack. Dust with confectioners' sugar.

HINT

• These little light cakes are lovely just dusted with confectioners' sugar, but you could make a glaze using the juice from the zested lemon, mixed to a thick paste with some sifted confectioners' sugar.

To store: Store in an airtight container for up to 2 days.

To freeze: Cool and freeze in an airtight container. Allow to defrost thoroughly before serving.

Lunchboxes

This was a tough chapter to write in the sense of trying to come up with really nice and tasty food that is also healthy. There is nothing harder than trying to force kids to eat healthily! So my solutions for creating a set of recipes that would appeal to children include roasting vegetables to increase flavor and sweetness, adding lower-fat cheeses such as mozzarella, and using slower energy-release foods, such as rice and pastas, in different ways. I have always been interested in using vegetables in sweet offerings as they add not only sweetness, but also texture: the Sweet Potato and Olive Oil Pecan Brownies (page 122) are a good example of this.

Banana bran muffins with streusel topping

This low-fat and high-fiber recipe is as delicious as the full-fat version.

1 heaping cup Gluten-free Flour
    Mix A (see page 19)

4½ tablespoons soft light brown
    sugar

1½ teaspoons gluten-free baking
    powder

½ teaspoon xanthan gum

½ teaspoon ground cinnamon

1 scant cup rice bran

2 eggs

2 tablespoons oil

2 medium bananas, mashed

½ cup skim milk

1 teaspoon vanilla extract

FOR THE TOPPING

1 tablespoon chopped walnuts or
    seed mix

1 tablespoon turbinado sugar

¼ teaspoon ground cinnamon

⅓ cup gluten-free banana chips,
    broken up

Preheat the oven to 350°F. Line a muffin pan with 12 paper muffin cases.

Mix together the ingredients for the topping and set aside.

For the muffins, in a large bowl mix together the flour, sugar, baking powder, xanthan gum, cinnamon, and rice bran. In another bowl mix the eggs, oil, mashed bananas, milk, and vanilla extract.

Make a well in the center of the dry ingredients and add the wet mixture. Stir gently until just combined, soft, and dropping from the spoon—don't leave it to stand after mixing. If the mixture is too dry, add a drop more milk.

Spoon the mixture into the paper muffin cases immediately, and top each muffin with the streusel topping. Bake for about 20 minutes until risen and golden.

The muffins are best served warm.

HINT
- The banana muffins can be enjoyed without the streusel topping, if you prefer.

To store: Store in an airtight container for up to 2 days. For best results, microwave for a few seconds to warm through before serving.

To freeze: Cool and freeze in an airtight container. Allow to defrost completely, and for best results, microwave for a few seconds to warm through before serving.

Roasted squash and basmati rice salad

A good, well-balanced salad, with plenty of vegetables and a nice, simple dressing—perfect lunchbox

SERVES: 8
PREPARATION: 20 MINUTES
COOKING: 25–30 MINUTES

⅔ cup frozen peas or beans
1 butternut squash, peeled and cut into bite-sized cubes
4 tablespoons olive oil
salt and freshly ground black pepper
4 medium tomatoes, roughly chopped
½ iceberg lettuce, finely sliced
1¼ cups cooked gluten-free basmati rice
4 tablespoons white wine vinegar
1 tablespoon granulated sugar
juice of 2 large limes
Freshly ground black pepper
4 tablespoons extra-virgin olive oil
1 bunch cilantro, roughly chopped

Cook the peas or beans according to the package instructions and drain.

Preheat the oven to 400°F.

Place the squash cubes in a baking pan, then add the olive oil and season well with salt and pepper, mix well, and roast for 25–30 minutes, until lightly browned and cooked through.

Meanwhile, place the tomatoes, cooked peas or beans, and chopped iceberg lettuce into a deep bowl, and mix carefully but well.

Remove the cooked squash from the oven and cool slightly. Leave to cool completely.

Add the squash to the tomatoes, beans, and lettuce, then add the rice. Spoon over the vinegar, sugar, lime juice, 1 teaspoon black pepper, the extra-virgin olive oil, and cilantro, then stir gently to combine thoroughly.

To store: Keep in the fridge for up to 2 days.
To freeze: Not suitable.

New potato, baby spinach, and mozzarella salad

This simple salad is a feast for the senses, and the dressing gives it a punchy overtone.

SERVES: 4
PREPARATION: 10 MINUTES PLUS COOLING
COOKING: 15–20 MINUTES

9 oz baby new potatoes
2 cups baby spinach leaves
4 oz mozzarella balls, drained

FOR THE DRESSING

4 tablespoons extra-virgin olive oil
1 tablespoon lemon juice
1 teaspoon whole grain mustard
½ garlic clove, crushed
pinch of sugar, optional

Boil or steam the potatoes until tender. Drain and set aside to cool.

Combine the ingredients for the dressing in a screw-top jar, and shake well (or whisk together in a small bowl).

Cut the cooled potatoes into quarters, and place in a large bowl. Add the spinach leaves and mozzarella.

Give the dressing another shake or stir, pour it over the salad and toss gently to combine.

HINT
- This would be equally good made with cubes of sweet potato and green beans, instead of potatoes and spinach.

To store: Keep in the fridge for up to 2 days.
To freeze: Not suitable.

Turkey pita breads

Turkey is so often underused—I think people are scared of cooking with it. Here is a nice way to cook turkey successfully, which results in an incredibly healthy meal.

12 oz turkey breast, diced

1 ripe avocado

juice of ½ lime

1 small garlic clove, crushed, optional

2 tomatoes, very finely diced

freshly ground black pepper

4 gluten-free pita breads or gluten-free rolls

chopped iceberg lettuce

First poach the diced turkey. Place it in a pan, pour over enough water to cover the turkey, partially cover with a lid, bring to a boil, then simmer for about 15 minutes, or until thoroughly cooked, and no pink remains. Drain well and cool.

Scoop the flesh from the avocado and mash until soft with the lime juice and garlic, if using. Add the diced tomato, mix well, and season with black pepper.

Split the gluten-free pita breads or rolls, and fill them with the turkey and avocado mixture and chopped lettuce.

HINTS

- You can use poached chicken breast instead of turkey. Follow the same poaching method as described above.
- For an alternative filling to the creamy avocado spread, simply mix equal amounts of gluten-free tomato ketchup and gluten-free mayonnaise together, and stir into the poached turkey pieces to coat.

To store: These are best served on the day they are made.

To freeze: Not suitable.

Pasta salad with cherry tomatoes and basil

A perfectly well-balanced salad that's easy to prepare and makes delicious lunchbox food.

18 oz (about 40) cherry or small
tomatoes

2 garlic cloves, thinly sliced

olive oil, for drizzling

11 oz gluten-free pasta shapes

small bunch of basil leaves,
roughly chopped

freshly ground black pepper

grated Parmesan or pecorino
cheese, to serve, optional

Preheat the oven to 400°F. Line a roasting dish with aluminum foil.

Remove the stalks from the tomatoes, and place in the lined dish. Mix the garlic slices in with the tomatoes, and drizzle with olive oil. Roast the tomatoes for about 20 minutes until the skins begin to color.

Cook the pasta according to the package instructions. Drain and keep warm.

Crush the tomatoes with a fork, drop in the basil leaves, and stir. Add the tomato mixture and all the cooking juices to the pasta. Season with black pepper. Drizzle over olive oil, and sprinkle with cheese, if using, to serve.

HINTS

- Roasting vegetables concentrates their natural sweetness and they are full of flavor, so there is no need to add any salt.
- Stir 2 tablespoons of half-fat crème fraîche into the tomato mixture, to make a more creamy sauce for the pasta.

To store: Keep in the fridge for up to 2 days.

To freeze: Not suitable.

Apple custard and yogurt fool

This is one of my absolute favorite flavor combinations—an autumnal delight.

2 medium Granny Smith apples, cored, pared and chopped into ½-inch pieces

¼ cup soft brown sugar

finely grated zest and juice of 1 lemon

2 oz gluten-free dark chocolate

10 gluten-free shortbread finger cookies, crumbled

2½ cups ready-made gluten-free lowfat custard*

2 scant cups Greek yogurt

Place the apples, brown sugar, lemon zest, and juice in a small pan. Bring to a boil, stirring occasionally, then turn down the heat and cook until the apples are soft and pulpy, about 15 minutes. You may need to add a little water if the mixture is too thick. Set aside to cool.

Grate the chocolate carefully on a fine grater, then chill well, or pop into the freezer.

Spoon half of the cooled apple into 6–8 small sealable plastic pots. Sprinkle the shortbread crumbs over the apple. Then spoon over half the custard and half the yogurt. Repeat with the remaining apple, custard and yogurt. Then finally sprinkle over the grated chocolate.

To store: Keep, covered, in the fridge for up to 2 days.

To freeze: Not suitable.

*If you can't find ready-made gluten-free lowfat custard, other options are canned custard, instant vanilla pudding and pie filling, or making up a quantity with custard powder (but check the ingredients to make sure it is gluten-free).

Sweet potato and olive oil pecan brownies

Adding vegetables to cakes has become more and more fashionable over the past few years. I often use pickled beets and also zucchini. Here the texture of sweet potato really adds to the gooeyness of the brownie.

2 medium sweet potatoes

oil, for greasing

5 oz gluten-free dark chocolate, chopped

scant ½ cup light extra-virgin olive oil

1 cup Gluten-free Flour Mix B (see page 19)

1 teaspoon gluten-free baking powder

¼ teaspoon xanthan gum

1¼ cups pecans, roughly chopped

2 large eggs

¾ cup soft brown sugar

Preheat the oven to 375°F.

Bake the sweet potatoes in their skins for about 45 minutes. When they are soft, slice them in half, and scoop out the flesh. Mash a scant 1¼ cups of potato flesh, and transfer it to a mixing bowl.

Increase the oven temperature to 400°F. Line an 8-inch square baking pan or dish with baking parchment, and oil well.

Place the chocolate and extra-virgin olive oil in a heatproof bowl over a pan of simmering water, or heat them gently in a microwave, until the chocolate melts.

Combine the gluten-free flour, baking powder, xanthan gum, and pecans together in another bowl.

Beat the warm chocolate and oil into the warm potato, and then add the eggs and sugar. Finally add the flour mixture and stir well.

Pour into the pan, and bake for about 30 minutes or until set and baked.

Cool slightly, and then cut into squares.

HINT

- This recipe is not recommended for younger babies because it contains nuts. Very occasionally babies can have a nut allergy, but they should be safe from 6 months.

To store: Keep in an airtight container for up to 2 days.

To freeze: Cool and freeze in an airtight container. Defrost completely before serving.

Snack Food

One of the subjects I get a huge number of comments and letters about is snack food. Most snacks are either packed full of, or coated in gluten-based products, making them a nightmare for celiac sufferers. In this chapter, I tackle the dearth of tasty gluten-free snack food. I offer fried snacks, such as Tortilla Chips (page 126), Polenta Zucchini Fries (page 129) and Plantain Chips with Dips (page 132). There is a also a simple, tasty lettuce-wrapped chicken dish (page 134), and even a posh version of cheese on toast with poached egg and spicy peppers (page 130).

Tortilla chips

When it comes to great snack food, celiac sufferers have a pretty raw deal. So here is a simple and tasty recipe. I think these crisp tortilla chips are much better than a lot of the offerings out there.

¾ cup Gluten-free Flour Mix A (see page 19)

2/3 cup fine gluten-free cornmeal (polenta)

¾ teaspoon xanthan gum

½ teaspoon gluten-free baking powder

salt

cornstarch, for dusting

vegetable oil, for deep-frying

chili powder, for dusting

Place the flour, cornmeal, xanthan gum, baking powder, and 2 pinches of salt in a bowl. Add enough warm water to form a soft dough—about ½ cup.

Remove from the bowl and knead well for 2–3 minutes, using a little dusting of cornstarch to stop the dough sticking to the work surface.

Divide the dough into 75 pieces—the smaller the pieces, the easier it is to roll them out.

Dust a rolling pin well with cornstarch, and roll out a piece of dough as thinly as possible into a square. Cut the square into 2 small triangles. Continue in this way with the rest of the dough pieces.

Heat the vegetable oil in a large pan to about 350°F (check the temperature using a thermometer or drop in a piece of bread; when it turns golden brown in 30 seconds, the oil is ready). Deep-fry the tortilla chips in small batches, until crisp on both sides. Drain well on paper towels, and dust with salt and chili powder to serve.

HINT

- These chips are good with a range of flavors. Try smoked or sweet paprika, Chinese five-spice powder, or ground chipotle chili powder and grated lime zest.

To store: Best served immediately.
To freeze: Not suitable.

Polenta zucchini fries with cream cheese dip

Most deep-fried foods are coated in bread crumbs or flour-based batters, making them a no-no for celiac sufferers. Here is a delicious way to eat a fried vegetable with a crunchy coating that is completely gluten-free.

4 medium zucchini

4–5 tablespoons cornstarch or
2–3 tablespoons arrowroot

½ cup milk

1⅔ cups fine gluten-free cornmeal
(polenta), the finer, the better

vegetable oil, for deep-frying

FOR THE DIP

9 oz gluten-free cream cheese

4–5 tablespoons milk

freshly ground black pepper

chili powder, optional

3–4 tablespoons chopped chives or
parsley

Make the dip by mixing the cream cheese and enough milk to give a soft dipping consistency. Season well with pepper and chili, if using, and then add the chives or parsley. Chill until ready to serve.

Dry the zucchini thoroughly on paper towels and cut them into ½-inch wide sticks.

Place the cornstarch or arrowroot into one bowl, the milk into another bowl, and the cornmeal into a third dish. Season the milk with a little pepper.

Dust the zucchini thoroughly, a few at a time, and then place into the milk. Dip in the cornmeal and turn to coat really well.

Repeat until all the zucchini are coated twice, and then dust off the excess.

Heat the vegetable oil in a large pan to about 350°F (check the temperature using a thermometer or drop in a piece of bread; when it turns golden brown in 30 seconds the oil is ready).

Deep-fry the zucchini in the hot oil in small handfuls (do not overfill the pan) until just cooked, and very lightly colored.

Season the zucchini fries with black pepper, and serve immediately, with the dip.

To store: Not suitable.
To freeze: Not suitable.

Cream cheese and Peppadew toasties with spinach and poached eggs

Tasty snack food at its best. These are easy to make and cook. I find that older kids like to try extreme flavors, so here is a classic example of that. Slightly spicy, sweet, and pickled all working well together.

7 oz gluten-free cream cheese

1 heaping cup finely grated Cheddar cheese

1 teaspoon gluten-free English mustard

4–5 Peppadew peppers (from a jar), drained and finely chopped

salt and freshly ground black pepper

2 egg yolks

4 slices gluten-free brown bread

4 fresh eggs

dash of vinegar

1 scant cup fresh spinach leaves

Preheat the broiler to medium.

Place the cream cheese, Cheddar, mustard, Peppadew peppers, salt and pepper into a bowl and mix really well. Add the egg yolks and stir thoroughly to combine.

Lightly toast one side of the bread slices. Spread the cheese mixture evenly over the untoasted sides of the bread.

Place on a baking sheet and broil until glazed and set perfectly—don't rush it.

Meanwhile, poach the eggs in simmering water with a dash of vinegar, and a pinch of salt.

Serve the toasties topped with a little fresh spinach and a soft poached egg.

To store: This is best eaten immediately.
To freeze: Not suitable.

Plantain chips with dips

A twist on a great snack—the unusual texture and flavor are a nice surprise. The dips are simple to make and really delicious.

SWEET CHILI TOMATO DIP

5 tablespoons gluten-free sweet chili sauce

5 tablespoons gluten-free tomato ketchup

1 tablespoon gluten-free mayonnaise

PEANUT DIP

¾ cup gluten-free smooth peanut butter

2 tablespoons gluten-free soy sauce

2 tablespoons lime juice

1 tablespoon honey

FOR THE CHIPS

2 plantains, about 14 oz

canola oil, for deep-frying

lemon juice and chili powder, to season

Mix all the ingredients for the sweet chili dip together and set aside.

Blend all the peanut dip ingredients together. Thin down with boiled water from the kettle until the mixture forms a dipping consistency. Set aside.

Peel the plantains and cut them at a slight diagonal into oval slices, as thinly as you can. Heat the oil in a deep pan until sizzling, and fry the plantain slices in batches for 3–5 minutes until golden. Lift out using a slotted spoon, and drain on paper towels.

Splash the plantain chips with lemon juice and sprinkle with chili powder. Serve the chips with the dips.

HINTS

- To season the chips, try a spice mix instead of the chili powder, such as Cajun spice mix.
- Sweet potato or cassava (manioc) can be used instead of plantain.
- The peanut dip is not recommended for children under the age of 3 because it contains honey and peanuts. Babies and toddlers are more likely to develop a food allergy if there is a family history of "atopy," for example, eczema, asthma, hayfever or food allergies. Very occasionally babies can have a nut allergy, but they should be safe from 6 months. Honey can cause a rare form of food poisoning in babies under 1 year.

To store: The chips are not suitable for storing. Keep the dips in airtight containers in the fridge for up to 2 days.

To freeze: Not suitable.

Roasted red pepper dip

Good powerful flavor here, and the longer you roast the peppers, the better the flavor will be. This dip also makes a good topping for pan-fried fish, or roasted chicken thighs, and keeps well.

2 large red peppers, quartered
   and seeded
oil, for roasting
1 fat garlic clove
⅔ cup plain yogurt
salt and freshly ground black
   pepper
vegetable crudités, to serve

Preheat the oven to 400°F. Coat the pepper quarters in a little oil, place in a small baking dish and roast them for 20–30 minutes. Allow to cool.

Put the peppers, including any cooking juices, with the garlic and yogurt, into a blender, and blend until smooth, or leave a little texture if you prefer. If the dip is too thick, add a little water, and stir well. Season to taste, and serve with the crudités.

To store: Keep in an airtight container in the fridge for up to 2 days.
To freeze: Not suitable.

Quick chicken iceberg parcels

A really great way to use up leftover chicken. Cook and place on the table, then let the family make the wraps themselves—great snack food.

1 tablespoon olive oil

1 small onion, finely chopped

1⅔ cups cooked chicken, finely chopped

⅓ cup canned or fresh water chestnuts, drained (if from a can) and finely chopped

scant ½ cup honey-glazed cashew nuts, finely chopped

4–6 tablespoons gluten-free Chinese plum sauce or gluten-free sweet chili sauce

2 tablespoons cornstarch

8 good-sized iceberg lettuce leaves

freshly ground black pepper

Heat the oil in a large frying pan, add the onion, and cook for 5 minutes.

Add the chopped chicken, water chestnuts, cashew nuts, and plum or chili sauce, and warm through.

Add a touch of water, and once it is boiling, thicken the sauce slightly, if necessary, with a paste made from the cornstarch and 4 tablespoons cold water. Add the paste gradually, stirring constantly, until the desired thickness is reached. Season well, transfer to a warmed bowl, and keep warm.

Place the lettuce leaves in a bowl.

To serve, place the bowl of chicken mix on the table with the bowl of lettuce leaves. Place a spoonful of mix into the center of each lettuce leaf, wrap well, and eat.

HINT

- This recipe is not recommended for younger babies because it contains honey-glazed nuts. Honey can cause a rare form of food poisoning in babies under 1 year. Very occasionally babies can have a nut allergy, but they should be safe from 6 months.

To store: Not suitable.

To freeze: Not suitable.

Apple caramel teacakes

In recent years there have been big improvements in the range of gluten-free products available from supermarkets. There are some excellent fruit breads around, and here is a lovely, tasty recipe that uses them perfectly.

heaping ¾ cup superfine sugar

scant ½ cup pecans

2 tablespoons heavy cream, optional

2 large Granny Smith apples, pared, cored and roughly chopped

grated zest and juice of 1 large lemon

2 gluten-free teacakes, halved*

Heat ½ cup of the sugar with just enough water to cover, about 5 tablespoons, in a small, heavy pan until the sugar dissolves. Boil rapidly until the sugar turns pale golden, and starts to brown. Then add the pecans and cook in the caramel for 15 seconds until lightly brown: not dark, or they will taste bitter.

Very carefully add 3 tablespoons water and the cream, if using, and then return to the heat to make a smooth sauce, stirring. Cool.

Place the apples, remaining sugar, the lemon zest, and juice in another small pan and cook for 10 minutes until the apples are nice and pulpy.

Lightly toast the teacake halves in a toaster. Top with the warm apple compote, and spoon over a little of the pecan caramel syrup, to serve.

HINT

- This recipe is not recommended for younger babies because it contains nuts. Very occasionally babies can have a nut allergy, but they should be safe from 6 months.

To store: Not suitable.

To freeze: Not suitable.

*A teacake is a bit like a slightly sweet hamburger bun with currants. You can substitute 4 slices of gluten-free raisin bread or 2 gluten-free hot cross buns.

Party Food

Here I cook foods that can be served at any party or gathering, whether for kids or grown-ups. The savory dishes range from a Gruyère quiche (page 144) and salmon skewers with a punchy dipping sauce (page 143) to a potato and cherry tomato tortilla (page 140) that can be eaten either hot or cold. There are recipes for the sweet-toothed too. The Gooey Chocolate Cake (page 148) is rich, and packed full of chocolate filling. Maple and Pecan Whoopie Pies (page 153) are soft, with a beautiful color and delicious toffee edge. I've also included that British teatime favorite, butterfly cakes, in a strawberry version (page 150), plus one of my weaknesses: Viennese Whirls (page 154).

SERVES: 4
PREPARATION: 15 MINUTES
COOKING: 35 MINUTES

Cherry tomato tortilla

This delicious and simple meal is really nice eaten hot or cold.

1¼ lb potatoes, sliced

3 tablespoons olive oil

1 onion, chopped

2 strips bacon, chopped

10 cherry tomatoes, halved

5 extra large eggs

freshly ground black pepper

Cook the potato slices in boiling water for 10 minutes and drain well.

Meanwhile, heat the oil in a nonstick, ovenproof frying pan, add the onion and bacon, and cook over medium heat for 10 minutes.

Add the potatoes and tomatoes to the pan, and continue to cook, stirring occasionally, until the potatoes begin to color, about 5 minutes.

Preheat the broiler to high.

Beat the eggs in a bowl, season with black pepper and pour over the potato mixture. Shake the pan gently to combine the ingredients evenly, and cook over low heat for a few minutes until the eggs begin to set at the bottom and sides.

Place the pan under the broiler, and cook the top briefly to set.

To serve, run a spatula around the edge, and invert the tortilla onto a plate. Cut into wedges to serve.

HINTS

- This is a brilliant way to use up leftover boiled or roast potatoes, and you can substitute the bacon with cubes of cooked ham.
- Instead of cooking the cherry tomatoes in the tortilla, you can serve them raw alongside, if you prefer.

To store: Not suitable.

To freeze: Not suitable.

Broiled salmon skewers with lime and ginger tamari dipping sauce

These flavors work superbly together—salmon is ideal, but monkfish also works really well.

4 × 5 oz skinless, boneless salmon fillets, cut into 1½-inch cubes

vegetable or olive oil, for frying

3½ oz instant gluten-free rice noodles, to serve

FOR THE MARINADE

4 tablespoons chopped fresh mint

zest and juice of 2 limes

4 tablespoons clear honey

½ teaspoon freshly ground black pepper

pinch of salt

1 tablespoon olive oil

FOR THE DIPPING SAUCE

½ small red onion, very finely chopped

1½ garlic cloves, very finely crushed

1 tablespoon very finely chopped fresh ginger root

3 tablespoons gluten-free tamari soy sauce

1½ tablespoons olive oil

1 teaspoon sugar

Thread the salmon cubes onto 8 small skewers and place on a plate or stainless-steel tray.

To make the marinade, combine all the ingredients in a bowl. Pour the mixture over the salmon, coat well, and set aside to marinate.

Meanwhile, make up the dipping sauce (the finer the ingredients are chopped, the better) by mixing all the ingredients together in a bowl really well.

When you are ready to cook, remove the salmon skewers from the marinade, and pat dry on paper towels. Heat a nonstick frying pan, and add a little vegetable or olive oil. Cook the salmon skewers for 3–4 minutes on each side, taking care not to overcook.

Add boiling water to the instant noodles, leave to soften for a few minutes and then drain well.

Divide the noodles between 4 plates and top each with 2 salmon skewers. Serve with a little dipping sauce spooned over, and offer the rest in a bowl separately.

HINT

- This recipe is not recommended for younger babies and toddlers because it contains honey, which can cause a rare form of food poisoning in babies under 1 year.

To store: Not suitable.
To freeze: Not suitable.

SERVES: 6–8
PREPARATION: 10 MINUTES
COOKING: 10–15 MINUTES
BAKING: 25–30 MINUTES

Bacon, leek, and Gruyère quiche

I like quiche, provided it's cooked correctly. I have had many very poor examples, and wanted to include one here that not only works and is very tasty, but is also a quiche that I have cooked for the best part of 30 years. I enjoy the flavor the bacon brings to the quiche, and I adore leeks.

1¼ cups milk

2 tablespoons vegetable oil

4 lean Canadian bacon strips, cut into small pieces

2 medium leeks, very finely chopped

2 garlic cloves, finely chopped

1 × 1½-inch deep, 9½-inch round gluten-free tart crust, blind baked (see page 19)

2 tablespoons roughly chopped fresh parsley

2 scant cups Gruyère cheese, grated

2 large eggs, plus 2 yolks

½ teaspoon grated nutmeg

freshly ground black pepper

green salad, to serve

Place the milk in a pan, bring it to a boil and allow it to cool slightly.

Preheat the oven to 350°F.

Heat the oil in a frying pan, add the bacon, and cook for about 10 minutes until crisp. Then add the leeks and garlic, and cook for another 5 minutes.

Spread the bacon mixture over the base of the tart crust while still in the pan. Sprinkle over the parsley, then top with the grated cheese.

In a pitcher, beat the eggs and egg yolks with the milk (remove any skin from the milk first), nutmeg, and black pepper.

Pour the egg mixture into the pastry-lined pan, but only half fill it. Place the pan on a baking sheet, then place it in the oven and carefully top up the quiche with the egg mixture. This way, you hopefully won't spill any.

Bake for about 25–30 minutes until set, and with a slight wobble in the center. Cool slightly before slicing. Serve with a crisp green salad.

To store: Keep in the fridge for up to 2 days and serve cold, or reheat thoroughly before serving.

To freeze: Cool and freeze in an airtight container. Defrost completely before reheating thoroughly.

Deep-fried beef with Chinese plum dipping sauce

Good, tasty party food! The beef can be cooked fresh and served hot, or prepared in advance and eaten cold.

9 oz beef filet, sliced horizontally, then cut into ¼-inch thick strips

2 teaspoons Chinese five-spice powder

4 tablespoons gluten-free Chinese yellow bean sauce

1 teaspoon finely chopped garlic

salt and freshly ground black pepper

vegetable oil, for deep-frying

1¼ cups cornstarch

superfine sugar, for sprinkling

1 jar (about 11 oz) gluten-free Chinese plum sauce, to serve

Toss the beef in the five-spice powder and yellow bean sauce. Add the garlic, mix well, and season with a touch of pepper. Leave to marinate for 15–20 minutes.

Heat the vegetable oil in a wok or deep pan to about 375°F (check the temperature using a thermometer or drop in a piece of bread; when it turns golden brown in 25 seconds the oil is ready).

Toss the beef in the cornstarch in batches, dust off well, then transfer it straight to the hot oil. Do not overfill the wok or pan, as the temperature of the oil lowers very quickly. Fry the beef until it is crisp but not crunchy, remove from the hot oil and drain on paper towels. Sprinkle with a little superfine sugar, and salt and pepper.

Serve the beef in small glasses, wrapped in napkins, with the Chinese plum dipping sauce offered separately.

To store: Not suitable.
To freeze: Not suitable.

Caramel sponge cake

This is a deliciously light vanilla sponge cake with an irresistible caramel cream filling.

vegetable oil, for greasing

1¾ cups + 1 tablespoon Gluten-free Flour Mix A (see page 19)

2 teaspoons gluten-free baking powder

1 teaspoon xanthan gum

2 sticks unsalted butter, at room temperature

1 teaspoon vanilla extract

1⅛ cups sugar plus extra for dusting

4 large eggs

3–4 tablespoons milk

FOR THE FILLING

heaping ½ cup superfine sugar

1¼ cups heavy cream

Preheat the oven to 350°F. Oil 2 × 8-inch layer cake pans and base-line with baking parchment.

Sift the flour, baking powder, and xanthan gum together and set aside.

In a large bowl, beat the butter, vanilla, and sugar for 2 minutes with an electric hand mixer until light. Next add the eggs, and fold the flour mixture in, until the batter is creamy. Stir in enough milk to make a soft mixture that drops from the spoon.

Divide the mixture between the pans and level the surface. Bake on the same shelf in the center of the oven for 25–30 minutes, until the sponge bounces back when touched.

Leave to cool slightly, and then remove from the pans onto a wire rack to cool completely.

To make the filling, heat the sugar and about 5 tablespoons water in a small, heavy pan over medium heat. Stir constantly until the sugar dissolves completely, including any grains on the sides of the pan. Boil rapidly until the sugar turns a golden caramel color (not too dark as this will taste bitter), and then remove from the heat: the syrup will continue to caramelize. Take great care because caramel reaches very high temperatures.

Add 6 tablespoons of the cream to the pan, and return to gentle heat, stirring, to make a smooth sauce. Cool, and then chill for 30 minutes.

Whip the rest of the cream separately, just until soft and thick. Fold into the cold caramel sauce.

Place one of the sponges onto a plate, and then spread the filling evenly over the cake. Top with the second sponge, and dust the top with a little superfine sugar, to finish.

To store: Store in an airtight container in the fridge for up to 2 days.

To freeze: Freeze the cake in an airtight container. Allow to defrost thoroughly before filling and serving.

Gooey chocolate cake

Chocolate in any form is a winner. The almonds make this cake nice and moist, and good-quality vanilla extract contributes to the rich chocolate hit.

MAKES: 1 × 8-INCH ROUND CAKE
PREPARATION: 25 MINUTES
BAKING: 50–60 MINUTES

vegetable oil, for greasing

1 ²/₃ cups Gluten-free Flour Mix B (see page 19)

1 teaspoon xanthan gum

2 teaspoons gluten-free baking powder

½ cup cocoa powder

1½ sticks unsalted butter, at room temperature

1 cup soft dark brown sugar

4 large eggs, beaten

1 teaspoon vanilla extract

1 cup milk

¾ cup ground almonds

FOR THE FILLING AND TOPPING

1 stick unsalted butter, at room temperature

1¾ cups sifted confectioners'sugar

½ cup cocoa powder, sifted

1 teaspoon vanilla extract or water

²/₃ cup gluten-free dark chocolate, grated

Preheat the oven to 350°C. Oil an 8-inch loose-based cake pan and base-line with baking parchment.

Sift the flour, xanthan gum, baking powder, and cocoa powder together.

In a deep bowl, beat the butter and the sugar together with an electric hand mixer, until light and fluffy. Gradually beat in the eggs and the vanilla.

Fold tablespoonfuls of the flour mixture into the butter and egg mix alternately with tablespoons of the milk, until the batter is evenly combined. Gently fold in the ground almonds. Add a little more milk if needed, so the mixture is soft and drops from the spoon.

Spoon the mixture into the pan and level the surface. Bake in the center of the oven for about 50–60 minutes until a skewer inserted in the center comes out clean. Leave to cool in the pan for 15 minutes, and then turn out onto a wire rack.

To make the filling and topping, beat the butter with the confectioners' sugar, cocoa powder, and vanilla, or enough water until you have a soft cream.

When the cake is completely cold, cut it in half horizontally, and then sandwich the halves together with half the chocolate cream. Spread the remaining cream over the top, and sprinkle with the grated chocolate.

Chill well, but remove from the fridge 30 minutes before eating, to bring the cake back to room temperature.

HINTS

- Microwaving a slice at a time for a few seconds will bring out the soft, gooey texture of this cake.
- This recipe is not recommended for younger babies because it contains nuts. Very occasionally babies can have a nut allergy, but they should be safe from 6 months.

To store: Store in an airtight container for up to 3 days in the fridge.

To freeze: Cool and freeze the filled and iced cake in an airtight container. Allow to defrost thoroughly before serving.

Strawberry jam butterfly cakes

Butterfly cakes have suddenly become really popular again, partly as a result of their promotion on TV baking programs. My mom made beautiful butterfly cakes, and so I was inspired to create a gluten-free version.

1½ sticks unsalted butter, at room temperature

heaping ¾ cup superfine sugar

1 teaspoon vanilla extract

1¼ cups Gluten-free Flour Mix A (see page 19)

1½ teaspoons gluten-free baking powder

½ teaspoon xanthan gum

2 large eggs, beaten, at room temperature

3 tablespoon milk

FOR THE BUTTERCREAM

1½ sticks soft unsalted butter

1¼ cups sifted confectioners' sugar, plus extra for dusting

1 teaspoon vanilla extract

2 tablespoons strawberry jam

Preheat the oven to 375°F. Line a muffin pan with 12 small paper cake cases.

Place the butter, sugar, and vanilla extract in a large bowl and beat together using an electric hand mixer.

Sift the flour, baking powder, and xanthan gum together.

Add 2 tablespoons of the flour to the creamed butter mixture, and stir to combine. Add the beaten eggs a little at a time, alternating with the flour, until it is all incorporated.

Stir in enough of the milk to produce a soft mixture that drops from the spoon.

Fill the paper cases almost to the top, and bake for 15–20 minutes until the cakes are well risen and golden. Remove from the oven, and cool on a wire rack.

For the buttercream, place the butter, confectioners' sugar, and vanilla in a large bowl and beat together using an electric hand mixer until you have a soft cream.

Using a sharp knife, slice the top off each cupcake, then cut the tops in half to make wings. Spoon a little strawberry jam into each cavity. Pipe or spoon the buttercream onto the jam, then place the two pieces of the cut circle at an angle onto the buttercream. Dust with confectioners' sugar and serve.

To store: These are best served on the day they are made.

To freeze: Freeze the cooled, unfilled cakes in an airtight container. Allow to defrost thoroughly before filling and serving.

Maple and pecan whoopie pies

I really like whoopee pies. They have a light sponge texture yet are very satisfying. The pecans here make a delicious variation.

1 heaping cup Gluten-free
    Flour Mix A (see page 19)

¼ teaspoon gluten-free baking
    powder

¼ teaspoon xanthan gum

¼ cup pecans, chopped

scant ½ stick margarine or butter

scant ½ cup soft dark brown sugar

1 teaspoon glycerine or corn syrup

1 teaspoon vanilla extract

1 large egg

2 tablespoons maple syrup

3½–7 tablespoons milk

FOR THE FILLING

⅔ cup heavy cream

1 tablespoon confectioners' sugar,
    sifted

2 tablespoons maple syrup

Preheat the oven to 350°F. Line 2 baking sheets with baking parchment.

Sift the flour, baking powder, and xanthan gum into a large bowl. Stir in the pecans.

In another bowl, use an electric hand mixer to beat the margarine, sugar, glycerine, vanilla, and egg together. Stir in the maple syrup.

Gradually stir the flour mixture into the creamed mixture, alternating with a little milk, and mix until smooth. Add enough milk to get the mixture quite soft, but still holding its shape.

Place small spoonfuls of the mixture in 16 mounds on the prepared baking sheets and flatten each slightly with your fingers: try to get them all a similar-sized round, about 2 inches in diameter. The cookies will spread to 2½–3 inches.

Bake for approximately 15 minutes until firm. Remove from the oven and cool on a wire rack.

To make the filling, whip the cream until soft and lightly thickened. Fold in the confectioners' sugar and the maple syrup.

Just before you are ready to serve, assemble the whoopies. Spread some cream over one flat side of a whoopie and sandwich with the other half.

HINT

- This recipe is not recommended for younger babies because it contains nuts. Very occasionally babies can have a nut allergy, but they should be safe from 6 months.

To store: These are best served on the day they are made.

To freeze: Freeze the cooled, unfilled whoopies in an airtight container. Allow to defrost thoroughly before filling and serving.

Viennese whirls

I first made these as a young apprentice, and I've always loved their soft and crumbly texture. They will expand slightly, so don't go mad on the piping.

2 sticks unsalted butter, at room temperature

heaping ½ cup sifted confectioners' sugar

1 teaspoon vanilla extract

2 large eggs

2⅓ cups Gluten-free Flour Mix A (see page 19)

¼ teaspoon xanthan gum

FOR THE FILLING

1¼ sticks unsalted butter, at room temperature

heaping ½ cup confectioners' sugar, plus extra for dusting

1 teaspoon vanilla extract

4 tablespoons raspberry jam, sieved

Preheat the oven to 350°F. Line 2 baking sheets with baking parchment.

Place the butter, sugar, and vanilla extract in a large bowl and use an electric mixer to beat them together until they are light and creamy. Next, beat in the eggs.

Sift the flour and xanthan gum together, and then fold the flour into the creamed mixture, until the mixture comes together (do not overbeat).

Fit a ⅝-inch star tip into a large piping bag and fill with the cookie dough. Pipe the mixture onto the prepared baking sheets. Pipe 24 small, round whirls, each about 2 inches in diameter. The cookies will spread to around 2½–3 inches. Bake for 15–20 minutes until firm through to the center. Remove from the oven, and cool on a wire rack.

To make the filling, place the butter in a bowl. Sift the confectioners' sugar and beat into the butter with the vanilla, until you have a soft cream.

Pipe or spread the flat side of each cookie with a little of the filling, dot with a little jam, and sandwich with another cookie. Place the whirls into paper cupcake cases and dust well with confectioners' sugar.

To store: These are best served on the day they are made.

To freeze: Freeze the cooled, unfilled cookies in an airtight container. Allow to defrost thoroughly before filling and serving.

DIRECTORY

CELIAC SOCIETIES

Your national coeliac society can provide more information about celiac disease, put you in touch with local groups, and keep you informed about events relating to celiac disease.

UNITED KINGDOM

Coeliac UK
3rd Floor Apollo Centre
Desborough Road
High Wycombe
Buckinghamshire HP11 2QW
Tel: +44 (0)1494 437278

Coeliac UK is the national charity for people with coeliac disease and dermatitis herpetiformis. You can contact Coeliac UK via their website at www.coeliac. org.uk or by phoning their Helpline on 0845 305 2060 (Helpline open 10–4, Mon, Tue, Thu, Fri and 11–4, Wed). The *Food and Drink Directory*, available in print and online, lists about 10,000 products that are safe to eat.

IRELAND

The Coeliac Society of Ireland
Carmichael House
4 North Brunswick Street
Dublin 7
Tel: +353 (0)1872 1471
www.coeliac.ie

USA

Celiac Disease Foundation
13251 Ventura Blvd Ste 1
Studio City, CA 91604
Tel: +1 818 990 2354
www.celiac.org

Celiac Sprue Association
PO Box 31700
Omaha, NE 68131-0700
Tel: +1 402 558 0600
+1 877 272 4272
www.csaceliacs.org

Gluten Intolerance Group
31214 124th Ave SE
Auburn, WA 98092-3667
Tel: +1 253 833 6655
www.gluten.net

American Celiac Society Dietary Support Coalition
PO Box 23455
New Orleans, LA 70183-0455
Tel: +1 504 737 3293
www.americanceliacsociety.org

CANADA

Canadian Celiac Association
5025 Orbitor Drive
Building 1, Suite 400,
Mississauga, ON L4W 4Y5
Tel: +1 905 507 6208
www.celiac.ca

Fondation Quebecoise de la Maladie Coeliaque
4837 rue Boyer, Bureau 230
Montreal, Quebec H2J 3E6
Tel: +1 514 529 8806
www.fqmc.org

AUSTRALIA

The Coeliac Society of Australia
PO Box 271, Wahroonga, NSW 2076
Tel: +61 2 9487 5088
www.coeliac.org.au

NEW ZEALAND

Coeliac Society of New Zealand
PO Box 35724, Browns Bay
Auckland 0753
Tel: +64 9 820 5157
www.coeliac.co.nz

GLUTEN-FREE PRODUCTS

If you are unable to find gluten-free products at your local supermarket or health-food shop, try the following online suppliers.

UNITED KINGDOM

Community Foods
Micross, Brent Terrace,
London NW2 1LT
Tel: +44 (0)208 208 2966
www.communityfoods.co.uk

Doves Farm Foods
Salisbury Road, Hungerford
Berkshire, RG17 0RF
Tel: +44 (0)1488 684880
www.dovesfarm.co.uk

Glutafin
442 Stockport Road
Warrington
Cheshire WA4 2GW
Tel: +44 (0)800 988 2470
www.glutafin.co.uk

Gluten Free Foods
Unit 270, Centennial Park
Centennial Avenue, Elstree
Borehamwood, Herts WD6 3SS
Tel: +44 (0)208 953 4444
www.glutenfree-foods.co.uk

Lifestyle Health Care Ltd
Mamhilad Technology Park
Pontypool NP4 0JJ
Tel: +44 (0)845 270 1400
http://gfdiet.com

IRELAND

Heron Quality Foods Ltd
Knockbrown Brandon
Co. Cork
Tel: +353 (0)233 9006
www.glutenfreedirect.com

Lavida Foods
UK Tel: +44 (0)844 774 5888
ROI Tel: +353 (0)61 458455
info@lavidafood.com
www.lavidafood.com

USA

Ener-G Foods
5960 First Avenue South
Seattle, WA 98108
Tel: +1 800 331 5222
www.ener-g.com

Gluten Free
www.glutenfree.com

Gluten Free Mall
www.glutenfreemall.com

Gluten Solutions
www.glutensolutions.com

Shop Organic
www.shoporganic.com

AUSTRALIA

Gluten Free Shop
553A North Road
Ormond, Victoria 3204
Tel: +61 3 9578 6400
www.glutenfreeshop.com.au

NEW ZEALAND

Gluten Free Goodies
Tel: +64 4 902 9696
www.glutenfreegoodies.co.nz

SOUTH AFRICA

Fresh Earth Food Store
103 Komatie Road
Emmarentia, Johannesburg
Tel: +27 11 646 3470
www.freshearth.co.za

INDEX